Wounded Saints

*The Secrets of
Elijah, Moses, David, Jeremiah,
Job, Jonah, Jesus, and Others Who
Triumphed over Emotional Pain*

Fran Sciacca

A Raven's Ridge Book

BAKER BOOK HOUSE
Grand Rapids, Michigan 49516

Scripture quotations, unless otherwise indicated, are taken from The Holy Bible, New International Version, copyright © 1973, 1978, 1984, International Bible Society. Used by permission of Zondervan Bible Publishers.

Scripture quotations marked RSV are taken by permission from the Revised Standard Version Bible, © 1946, 1952, 1971, 1973 National Council of Churches of Christ in the U.S.A., New York, New York.

Scripture quotations marked NASB are taken by permission from the New American Standard Bible, © 1960, 1962, 1963, 1968, 1971, 1973, 1975, 1977, The Lockman Foundation, La Habra, California.

ISBN: 0-8010-8341-9

Printed in the United States of America

92 93 94 95 96 97/10 9 8 7 6 5 4 3 2 1

CONTENTS

Preface: Does God Love Cracked Pots? 9

Introduction: Two Ways of Seeing 17

1. Elijah: Backslidden or Burned Out? 25

2. Elijah: The Cause and Cure of Burnout 37

3. Moses: Unwillingness to Delegate Responsibility 61

4. Asaph: The Foul Fruit of Comparison 79

5. David: Dealing With Guilt 93

6. David: Dealing With False Guilt 105

7. Israel: Looking to the Past 119

8. Jeremiah: Looking for Success 131

9. Job: When the Lights Go Out 145

10. Job: Walking in Darkness 159

11. Jonah: Pride and Anger 175

12. Jesus: Facing Rejection 191

13. Barnabas: Encouragement—
       The Alternative to Self-Preoccupation 209

For a "wounded saint"
who reflects the character of Jesus
when most others would have followed
the counsel of Job's wife.
I dedicate this book to my good friend
Jon Stine.

PREFACE

Does God Love Cracked Pots?

We are immersed in an epidemic of emotional pain. Everywhere we turn we come face to face with someone who either is hurting deeply or has just emerged from some intense personal trial. A survey of one adult Sunday school class revealed that 50 percent of the members had been, or were currently in therapy. Words like *dysfunctional, co-dependence,* and *syndrome* are no longer the eclectic language of trained professionals. They permeate and even dominate common conversation among Christians. What has happened? Why, according to William Kirk Kilpatrick, has the membership of the American Psychiatric Association risen 400 percent in the last twenty-five years? A Christian friend who is also a professional counselor told me that a substantial percentage of the clients she sees do not need to be there. Why, then, do they come?

There are a number of very reasonable explanations. But before I address them, let me say by way of disclaimer that I wholeheartedly believe in the necessity and validity of professional counseling. Solving some people's traumas is harder than unscrambling an omelette. Others have organic or congenital disorders that an untrained eye would not only miss, but could compound by foolishly diagnosing it as purely a spiritual problem. There are too many Christians with hypoglycemia, for instance, who until proper diagnosis were exhorted to the point of exhaustion by well-meaning Christians.

There exists a need and a place for counselors who are solid in their Christian faith. But what about the large number of Christians who are in therapy for no legitimate reason? Why are they there?

There are four key reasons:

The first is a growing loss of confidence in the relevance and authority of Scripture as a *first choice* resource for comfort, insight, and guidance. With the rise in sources of "vicarious Bible study" (Christian radio teaching, the "tele-church," audio and video cassettes), many of us no longer experience the power and joy of first-hand encounters with the Spirit of God in his Word.

Instead, we settle for someone else's convictions, someone else's study, someone else's joy. But vicarious learning can never produce the confidence in God's competence that comes from personal familiarity with Scripture. David said, "Your statutes are my delight; they are my counselors" (Ps. 119:24), and, "I have more insight than all my teachers, for I meditate on your statutes" (Ps. 119:99). Every year at Christmas we proclaim, "And he will be called Wonderful Counselor, Mighty God . . ." (Isa. 9:6). Jesus said of the Holy Spirit, "And I will ask the Father, and he will give you another Counselor to be with you forever—the Spirit of truth." (John 14:16–17)

God intended from the very beginning that *he* would be our primary counselor, our source of diagnosis, insight, and guidance. And the primary vehicle of that desired ministry of God is the Scriptures. Paul affirms this in Romans 15:4:

> For everything that was written in the past was written to teach us, so that through endurance and the encouragement of the Scriptures we might have hope.

God's primary purpose in providing the Bible is of course to reveal himself to us. But a secondary purpose is insight, encouragement and guidance—the elements that comprise counseling.

The frenetic pace of our culture prevents sufficient time to reflect on the revelation of God in Scripture. I vividly recall the direct mail marketing ploy of one publisher. The brochure proclaimed, "Most Christians don't have time in their busy schedules to sit and read the Bible. But now you can take God's Word with you wherever you go!" The ad was for the Bible on audio cassette. Sadly, it captured the dilemma succinctly: We don't read God's Word.

In an era when we are tempted to make time alone with God merely another scheduled event on our daily treadmill, listening to Scripture while I run, commute, or pay the bills is a welcome substitute for reading and studying Scripture *while I meet with God.* The tragedy is the distance that slowly develops between me and the author of Scripture. Lacking his available comfort and guidance, in times of desperate need I may choose to seek "professional help."

A second reason for the proliferation of therapy as a Christian's first choice is a strange and relatively modern belief in our own incompetence. We live in an era when God could easily destroy the earth with another flood . . . of information! The amount of information available to each and every individual increases exponentially every minute. Computer ads show business people drowning in seas of paperwork, and offer programs to help handle all the data.

The unfortunate result of all this is the erroneous conclusion that because I can never know it all, I can never know *enough.* People are thoroughly convinced that they cannot adequately care for their own finances, their own marriage, their own children, their business, and above all, themselves. And this feeling of incompetence has given birth to a new breed of individual—the specialist!

Most of us are inundated regularly with the message that, "I am incompetent outside of my specialty." So when there is a problem child, a stagnation in our marriage, a mid-life reevaluation of our goals and direction, we feel pressured to seek "professional help." Just recently a Christian radio station ran an ad for a Christian counseling center in which they very dramatically portrayed problems with in-laws, a child getting poor grades, and low self-esteem as "crises" demanding professional help.

An even more unfortunate consequence of this incompetency mindset is that we do not believe we can substantially help each other. My wife, Jill, and I recently spent an evening with a couple whose marriage was in trouble. They had been in therapy individually and jointly for two years. Both were college graduates and very successful in their work. They believed that their marriage was "over" because they had been in therapy and, "If that hasn't helped, what could?" Jill and I looked at each other, thinking we had gotten in over our heads this time. But as we shared dinner we tried to reassure them that God wanted to glorify himself in their weakness. We also told them how we go on a weekly "date"— to talk, pray, and listen together.

They both panicked. "What do you talk about for an entire evening!"

Sparing you the lengthy details, let me just report that, a year later, that couple now goes out on a date each week—and their marriage is pulsing with life and hope! Why? I believe it is because Jill and I were faithful to the clear teaching of Hebrews 10:25:

> Let us not give up meeting together, as some are in the habit of doing, but let us encourage one another . . .

The Greek word used here for *encourage* means to "keep someone on their feet, who, if left to himself would collapse." Certainly the advice Jill and I gave that couple is not a foolproof success formula for every troubled marriage. Yet God has equipped each of us, in Christ, with the ability to help "keep one another on our feet." And he has commanded us to do that. Jill and I were merely acting in obedience to that command.

A third reason we are preoccupied with professional help is the disintegration of the concept of accountability. In a culture that seems to deify the individual, even as Christians we are tempted to forget that we are "members together of one body" (Eph. 3:6). The cultural principle of the right of privacy has infiltrated the church—so much so that many elder boards live in fear of legal retribution for exercising church discipline. I sat with a close friend a short time ago and asked him if he would hold me accountable for a couple areas of my life that I simply could not get under control. His response saddened and stunned me: "Fran, I'm just not into keeping tabs on people. I think that's too legalistic."

Hebrews 3:13 makes mutual accountability more than a suggestion:

> But encourage one another daily, as long as it is called Today, so that none of you may be hardened by sin's deceitfulness.

When we fail to hold one another accountable, it fosters the mindset that *my* Christian life is none of *your* business. In this context, a therapist becomes a very safe, neutral third party, much like the priest who heard my confessions as a Catholic youth. He was separated from me by a thin veil, so that even though he knew my personal moral failures he was kept a safe distance from my day-to-day existence. Confession always made me feel good, but rarely did it produce any long-term changes in my behavior.

A final and I believe primary reason we pursue unnecessary professional help is our preoccupation with perfection. Self-improvement is the idol of our day. The last time I checked, almost half of the top twenty video titles were for fitness workouts! We eat cereals that we hate because they'll reduce our chances of cancer. We wear clothing that almost glows in the dark to convince us we are serious about jogging. We are surrounded by friends who are "working on" one thing after another. Some of us even believe that when the Bible speaks of sanctification it really means self-improvement.

God's program for our lives is not self-improvement, but selflessness. John the Baptist captured what should be our central focus: "He must become greater; I must become less" (John 3:30). Sanctification and self-improvement are not synonyms. In fact, sanctification may in some cases actually demand that what we want to "work on" be left the way it is.

The example of Paul's life in 2 Corinthians 12:1–10 illustrates this radical truth. Whether his "thorn in the flesh" was a physical ailment or an emotional weakness isn't essential. The point is that, what Paul wanted to take *out* of his life, God wanted to leave *in*—for the express purpose of producing humility and dependence on God. Paul alluded to this principle earlier, in chapter 4:

> But we have this treasure in jars of clay to show that this all-surpassing power is from God and not from us. We are hard pressed on every side, but not crushed; perplexed, but not in despair; persecuted, but not abandoned; struck down, but not destroyed. We always carry around in our body the death of Jesus, so that the life of Jesus may also be revealed in our body. For we who are alive are always being given over to death for Jesus' sake, so that his life may be revealed in our mortal body. So then, death is at work in us, but life is at work in you. (vv. 7–12)

Paul compared us to clay pots. He might just as well have called us "cracked" pots. And his point is that God actually chooses to work with flawed vessels, in order to confirm the divine source of his power. Just as the Lord allowed Paul to keep his thorn in the flesh, those thorns in your own life—the things you are forever "working on"—may be there for a purpose.

These four assumptions—that Scripture need not be our first choice for counsel; that we are incapable of handling our own problems; that we are not accountable to our fellow believers; and that we must strive for perfection—underlie much of the present notion that "professional help" should be a Christian's first choice when facing any difficulty. If these assumptions have become unconscious convictions in your own life, there is a way out.

If you have strayed from giving first priority to God's Word, you can easily remedy that. Purpose today that you will begin afresh. Perhaps a study guide would provide you with the necessary structure and direction as you seek to recultivate your familiarity with and confidence in the Bible. Most of all, ask God to make his Word your first counselor. Be creative, but be serious. Spend time *alone* with God.

Perhaps you feel incompetent and insignificant. Ask God to direct someone into your life whom *you* can help. Be alert. Be available. Be attentive. Focusing for awhile on another person's pain can help you escape the downward spiral of your own problems:

> And if you spend yourselves in behalf of the hungry
>   and satisfy the needs of the oppressed,
> then your light will rise in the darkness,
>   and your night will become like the noonday. (Isa. 58:10)

Is there someone in your fellowship grieving the loss of a spouse or child? Perhaps your neighbor has lost his job? Give of yourself to such people.

Maybe you have developed a "Lone Ranger" approach to the Christian life. People love, respect, and appreciate you, but they're never allowed to "look under the mask" to the real you. Many of the tragedies in Christian leadership in recent years can be traced to a lack of accountability. I recently attended a seminar where the leader exhorted the attendees to form "E-Teams" (encouragement teams) for the purpose of discipline, encouragement, and accountability. I finally have a group of men doing for me what my one friend refused to do—holding me accountable in my problem areas. At last I have a real hope for victory in those areas.

An E-Team doesn't need to be a group. Jill is much more private than I am, so she prefers to meet weekly with one other woman for Bible study, and they are accountable to each other. It's also an excellent way to assure that they both regularly spend time in the Scriptures.

Finally, perhaps you realize that you've become so preoccupied with self-improvement that you've slowly become self-centered. A wise Christian told me, "Strengthen your strengths, and bring your weaknesses up to a tolerable level." Good counsel!

Again, this book is not intended to be a "word from the mountain" on how to solve all your problems in one afternoon. Some people do need professional help, and counseling does play a necessary role in God's economy. But there is also a valid place for the truth that in Christ we can be confident that he can help us, competent to help each other, and assured that, indeed, God can use cracked pots!

INTRODUCTION

Two Ways of Seeing

When Jill and I were living in Denver during my seminary years, our primary source of income was managing two apartment complexes. It would be an understatement to say that we learned more from our interaction with the menagerie of residents who populated those buildings than I ever accumulated from studying biblical anthropology. It was a crash course in "Humanity 101."

Jill became especially close with one of the tenants, a girl nicknamed Mickey. Mickey had grown up in a conservative Christian home, but had long since abandoned her faith in God. During our year-and-a-half as managers, Mickey and Jill exchanged countless stories. One in particular stands out in light of this book's theme. Mickey's younger sister had married quite young. Within two years of her wedding she was divorced. Mickey told us that she and her sister had never heard or seen their parents fight. Consequently, they both grew up believing that Christian couples don't fight. Needless to say, Mickey's sister had her theology rearranged within a week of her wedding. But because she grew up believing Christian couples don't fight, she concluded that her marriage, because it included conflict, couldn't possibly be God's will . . . so she divorced her husband!

This rather extreme example is an excellent illustration of a larger principle: What we *believe* about life will determine how we go about trying to live it. Our expectations have a tremendous impact on our sense of fulfillment and satisfaction in general, but particularly in the arena of human relationships.

A Romantic View of Life

One popular view of life insists on seeing it as it "ought" to be. Those who embrace this particular perspective have enshrined an idealized and inflated view of people, including themselves. This romantic view of life demands near-perfection from people, particularly people in positions of leadership. This view is often amplified in the Christian world. We go from indignation to embarrassment to anger whenever we hear of a Christian leader who has committed a grievous sin. While it is true that sin is always serious, and public sin often has more serious consequences, the fact that we are "shocked" by sinful behavior reveals that our understanding of people, even God's people, is too romantic and unrealistic.

Turning a romantic view of people inward on ourselves can have the most tragic consequences of all. When we establish standards for our own attitudes and behavior that are loftier than human nature allows, we set ourselves up for certain disappointment. The late Francis Schaeffer put it best when he said, "If I demand perfection from myself, then I will destroy myself."[1]

A romantic view of people, one that demands that I and others meet certain unwritten standards, yields a life of constant dissatisfaction and dashed expectations. And it forces me to deny the very emotions that result from the relational failures such a view produces. My true feelings are placed in subordination to how one "ought" to feel.

---

[1]Francis A. Schaeffer, *No Little People* (Downers Grove, Ill.: InterVarsity, 1974), 48.

A Realistic View of Life

On the other hand, we can espouse a view of life and people that is honest with the facts. Christians, of all people, should have a realistic view of life. For we claim to believe the doctrines of original sin and the depravity of man. We know that the unpopular concept of sin is central to understanding life, particularly human relationships. We understand that sin has infected every area of our existence. It has stained every relationship, tarnished every motive, blighted every natural ability, and touched every person. We, more than anyone else, know that human beings are sinners, and that as such they will fail us and will fail themselves.

A realistic view of life and of people does not minimize or excuse sin, yet it also does not ignore the pervasive effect of sin and what it really means to be a sinner. Having a realistic view of people will dramatically color my expectations of others. It will also have an impact on the way I view myself and consequently on how I treat myself.

This realistic view of human nature is the outlook of God himself. If we were given the assignment of writing biographies of selected servants of God, most of us would be tempted to edit the stories quite a bit. We would want to overlook or at least minimize their shortcomings. God is so unlike us! He weaves into the fabric of the Bible threads of failure as well as success. We are confronted with cowardice, treason, fatalism, depression, fatigue, pride, and insensitivity— even suicide! These unsavory character traits appear right alongside courage, conviction, faithfulness, and hope. In fact, God is so realistic in his portrayal of humanity that, in the words of Schaeffer, the Bible "is almost embarrassing at times."[2]

It is embarrassing because God's realism affects the stories of people we would prefer to keep on their pedestals. We have no difficulty discussing the failures of those we have already labelled as

---

[2]Schaeffer, *No Little People* , 49.

losers. People like Judas Iscariot, King Saul, Jezebel, and Pontius Pilate are nefarious no-goods whose vile conduct suits their character. But what about "righteous Lot," who in a drunken stupor had sex with both of his daughters? Or Jacob, the man who made a career out of deceit? Elijah became so depressed he wanted to die. And Jonah was so controlled by selfish pride that he was totally blind to God's love, and was willing to let an entire city perish rather than preach forgiveness.

The sad truth is that, all too often, *Christians actually have a romantic view of the Bible!* We don't really believe that the heroes of the faith were actually people just like us. Yet the Bible is full of relevant truth for today in its accounts of men and women who loved God deeply even though they failed him significantly.

The Bible is realistic, not romantic in its presentation and understanding of people. It is ruthlessly honest. James says that the prophet Elijah was "a man just like us" (James 5:17), or in the words of the Living Bible, "Elijah was as completely human as we are." We have no difficulty affirming that description in reference to Elijah's good example of faith and prayer, which is the immediate context of the verse. But was Elijah someone "just like us" in his weaknesses too? Did he cry? Did he become angry and afraid like us? Did he ever want to "throw in the towel"? Did he ever want to *die*, rather than live? The answer to all those questions is yes. Elijah, a hero in the family of God, wasn't a man of steel. He was a real person. The Bible does not give us romantic portraits, because that's not the way God sees us.

In Romans 15:4 Paul tells us that, "through endurance and the encouragement of the Scriptures"—in part, through the example of very human people like Elijah—we can have hope. James and Paul would agree that life—especially life as a Christian—is hard; you and I will often be tempted to quit. But they would also agree that there *are* answers to the struggles we face, and those answers are in God's Word. If we will expose ourselves to the Scriptures, study the character of God and how he dealt with these men and women who were "just like us," we'll discover how they endured the same temptations, failures, and sins that haunt us.

Wounded Saints will help you see that the Bible is adequate to meet most of your personal emotional needs, as it reveals real people dealing with real-life situations—with the help of a real God. *Wounded Saints* will take you into the files of biblical "case studies" of people who were either depressed or caught in depressing circumstances, or both. But before we begin, it's vital for you to determine which perspective *you* have on people—the romantic or the realistic perspective. And the best way to find that out is to investigate three common fallacies regarding the whole issue of depression and the Christian.

Is Depression Bad?

The apostle Paul warned Timothy, "But mark this: There will be terrible times in the last days" (2 Tim. 3:1). And he went on to specifically predict that, in those "last days" people would love themselves more than others, money more than integrity, and revenge more than forgiveness. The smallest package in the world is someone wrapped up in himself. People who are chronically depressed are usually self-absorbed. No one enjoys being around someone who is emotionally down all the time. They "rain on our parades" and get on our nerves. In a culture where recreation and leisure have become shrines of pleasure, "fun" people are more attractive.

When you combine with this the stigma attached to *Christians* who are depressed, emotional pain and difficulty quickly become things to hide. After all, if I claim to have a relationship with God but still struggle with bouts of depression and discouragement, it certainly seems to suggest that God is not my total sufficiency.

Many Christians feel an amorphous sense of responsibility to hold up a positive image to the watching world . . . or at least to the watching church. Somewhere in our pilgrimage, we have adopted the twisted notion that a "victorious Christian" resembles the happy groom in the receiving line at his wedding, exultant and eternally smiling. Joy becomes synonymous with jubilance.

Yet as we shall see, great men and women of God were sometimes seriously depressed. And their emotional storms were not merely slight disruptions on their spiritual landscape. They were as discouraged and down as you or I will ever be. It was not unusual for those deeply in love with God to despair of life itself. In fact, there actually seems to be some correlation between how closely one walks with the Lord and how intensely they battle their own emotions. This doesn't mean, of course, that depression is a sign of spiritual maturity. But it does verify that genuinely godly people can face, battle, and endure deep emotional and spiritual struggles.

To believe that depression is symptomatic of second-class spirituality is the product of a romantic view of life.

To Whom Can I Turn?

A second indicator of misunderstanding about the place of discouragement and depression in the Christian life is evidenced by where we tend to go when we are discouraged. As we have noted, Christian counseling is presently enjoying a heyday. More Christians want to see counselors than there are Christian counselors to see them. This is partly due to the failure of Christians to simply reach out and take an interest in each other. But it is also due, as noted, to the growing conviction that we are incompetent to deal with specialized areas of our own lives. We live in an age of specialists—men and women who can do for us what we believe we can no longer do for ourselves. And chief among our "inadequacies" is our inability to discern what is wrong with us and prescribe a course of remedial action.

The message of the Bible stands in stark contrast to this modern notion. God tells us that through "endurance and the encouragement of the Scriptures" we can have hope. There is ample help for most of our problems in the Word of God. More and more of us are spending less and less time reading, studying, and praying over the pages of the Bible. And in so doing, we widen the gap of credibility between God's Word and our problems. We miss the opportunity for *God* to tell us what is wrong, what is right, and how to know the difference.

Don't Worry . . . Be Happy?

A third indicator that we are misunderstanding discouragement and depression has to do with where we look for happiness. Adrift from absolute values, and dependent upon needy people to exist, much of modern psychology is motivated by the goal of making clients *feel* better. This is evident in the titles of books like *Feeling Good: The New Mood Therapy,* by David Burns. People want their feelings to change, especially their feelings about themselves. That is the underlying motivation for most who seek professional help.

This is unfortunate at best and tragic at worst, because it is an unattainable goal. In the Sermon on the Mount, Jesus said, "Blessed [happy] are those who hunger and thirst for righteousness, for they will be filled" (Matt. 5:6). In those words lies an incredibly powerful principle, one that swims against the tide of today's rush for relief: The person who sets his or her heart on being like God (righteousness) is the one who will be satisfied and happy. In other words, happiness is a *byproduct*. It is the fruit of pursuing godliness. It cannot be attained by itself. It is the result of seeking to know God and to become like Christ.

This shouldn't surprise us. From Romans 8:29 we learn that God has predestined us to become like Jesus Christ. If that is our destiny, carved out for each of us by a God of love, it shouldn't surprise us that it is also the path to happiness.

But the current emphasis on seeking personal happiness puts the biblical call for godliness on the shelf. Not only is this a serious deviation from the plans and purposes of God, it is also an exercise in futility. Trying to help people secure something that God has said is outside their grasp will be about as successful as trying to produce eggs without chickens.

This does *not* mean that God wants us unhappy and miserable, so that he can take credit for any joy we might find. It does mean, however, that a realistic view of life demands that we acknowledge we are made in the image and likeness of God, and that our personal joy and fulfillment comes from our relationship with him.

A realistic view of life and people admits that depression is real, that it is not an indicator of second-class spirituality. God's intention in the midst of depression is that we seek *him*, not happiness. In the process of doing this, we will obtain both God *and* happiness. But if we set our hearts on happiness instead of God, we will end up with neither.

ONE

Elijah:
Backslidden or Burned Out?

She sat at the kitchen table, the stone-cold coffee rippling as each new tear fell from her red and puffy eyes. Why? Why did she feel this way? God seemed a million miles away, if he existed at all. Her Bible lay open before her as it had yesterday and the day before. The more she tried to find God the more elusive he seemed. What was the use? Christianity seemed like little more than a religious habit, devoid of any real power.

Peggy couldn't remember the last time she had felt encouraged. Ever since the doctor told her and Tim that she was pregnant for the third time, their lives had seemed to become a suffocating and empty existence. Her thoughts stumbled over each other in search of a place to rest and find meaning. But that too was interrupted by Jason's cough and predictable crying. Why couldn't she cope? God had blessed her with a loving husband and three lovely children. It was the model Christian family, the model Christian home. Yet her prayers seemed to stick in the ceiling tiles; her Bible had become a collection of empty phrases. She and Tim were fighting more, as he sought to cope with this depression that eluded description and cure. Where was her faith? Where was her joy? Why did she continually have to fight back thoughts of suicide? She felt like an ungodly, shallow, and faithless Christian.

The above story is fictional, but it's also true. It is the story of hundreds of mothers at home, women on the go, fathers, teachers, pastors, and college students. It is the story of people who honestly wish they were in love with God, but aren't. They are convinced that their faith is offensive to him, that its dimly burning wick will soon be extinguished.

Depression like this is deceitful, not because of what it is but because of what it isn't. Too often, what we conclude is a hopeless spiritual condition, evidence of a faithless heart, is really only the natural consequences of a life that is over-extended. It is the fruit of burnout, not backsliding.

One of the clearest and most encouraging examples of this type of depression is the Old Testament prophet Elijah. A careful study of his life provides us with precious insight and principles for healing and recovery. First, we'll examine the *apparent* cause of Elijah's deep discouragement. Then we'll take a closer look at what I believe was the actual cause. Finally, we'll discuss some of the practical lessons we can learn from Elijah, some specific steps we can take to undo damage already done by depression in our own lives, and how we can prevent further pain.

Elijah makes his official debut in the Bible in the first verse of 1 Kings 17:

> Now Elijah the Tishbite, from Tishbe in Gilead, said to Ahab, "As the LORD, the God of Israel, lives, whom I serve, there will be neither dew nor rain in the next few years except at my word."

Elijah simply "appears" in the biblical text. There is no introduction, no apparent background or description of this prophet. But the surrounding context in 1 Kings provides us with rich insight about this mighty man of God. In chapter 18 another prophet, Obadiah, encounters Elijah one day in a field. Obadiah is surprised to see him. Elijah tells Obadiah to go to King Ahab and ask him to come to Elijah. Obadiah panics: "'What have I done wrong,' asked Obadiah, 'that you are handing your servant over to Ahab to be put to death?'" (v. 9)

The famine that had plagued the land for three years was the result of Elijah's prayers, and Ahab had been searching for him ever since, to kill him. Obadiah told Elijah he was afraid that, as soon as he went to get the king, Elijah would "disappear" like he had done repeatedly in the past, and in his anger Ahab would kill Obadiah. We can see from this encounter that Elijah was no stranger to Israel. In fact he had been around quite a while, and had earned the reputation of one who knew God intimately and walked with him faithfully. Elijah was a seasoned, experienced prophet of God.

He was also one who had witnessed miracle after miracle, from being fed by ravens near a brook, to seeing the never-ending supply of grain and oil at the widow of Zarephath's house. He had seen his prayers bring on a famine and raise a young boy from the dead.

He was also apparently very important to God. He is the one prophet who "has a foot in" both the Old and New Testaments. The last book of the Old Testament ends with the prediction that Elijah will return, and the New Testament opens with the appearance of John the Baptist, whom Jesus tells us is the fulfillment of that prophecy. It is Elijah who, along with Moses, ministers to Jesus during his transfiguration near Caesarea Philippi. Can you imagine how we would promote such a man if he were leading a week of preaching at our church!

A Prophet in Hiding

But the man who stands before us in the very next chapter (1 Kings 19) is drastically different. Here we find our mighty prophet of God hiding out in the Judean countryside because a woman had told him that she was going to reduce him to "dead meat" within twenty-four hours. There were 900 false prophets lying dead in the plains of Jezreel, thanks to Elijah, and Jezebel had vowed, "God do so to me if within the next day you're not like them!"

Suddenly, the prophet who had challenged the pagan religious establishment of an entire nation, and had seen God's power in a display nearly unparalleled in Scripture, is hiding under a tree, wanting to die! Surely James was right. Elijah was truly a man "of like nature with ourselves" (James 5:17, RSV). Every one of us who has ever been deeply depressed can identify with him.

Elijah is depressed. In fact, he's despondent! Why? What can cause a man of this spiritual stature to crater and want to quit? The apparent cause is Jezebel, the wicked wife of weak King Ahab who has pronounced the death sentence on Elijah. He is petrified. Upon hearing that Jezebel is going to kill him he immediately, "ran for his life. When he came to Beersheba in Judah, he left his servant there, while he himself went a day's journey into the desert. He came to a broom tree, sat down under it and prayed that he might die." (1 Kings 19:3–4)

Most of us have been there. "Lord, I've had enough! Take my life. I'm no better than my ancestors" (see v. 4). It's a gnawing sense of hopelessness, with no relief in sight. The conviction that you simply can't go on any longer. And it is all compounded by an overwhelming sensation of spiritual impotence, a vacuum in your life where God once was.

The apparent cause of Elijah's depression is obvious. Jezebel has threatened his life and he is buckling under the pressure. She has the power to fulfill her every wish. It's easy to understand Elijah's fear.

Imagine for a moment that Elijah is a close friend of ours. We graduated from the same college, or work together, or are neighbors. We've just heard that our friend has checked into a local motel and apparently is planning to kill himself. In desperation we drive to the motel, knock on his door, and walk in. He's sitting on the edge of his bed, staring out the window at the traffic. After we've small-talked and he's given us the background as to why he is sitting there, what would we say to him? Would we try to talk about the good times? "Elijah, look how God has used you. Think back on how real God has been in your life."

Maybe our friend Elijah has had some major impact in our own life. Would we say, "Elijah, look at me. I'm living proof that you have been a useful servant of God."

Would we try to get him to ignore his feelings? Or would we resort to a subtle form of manipulation? "Elijah, your witness is at stake here. I can understand how you feel, but if you go down the pipe, it will really hurt the Christians who have supported you. You've been in their pulpits. You've preached to them. Think of how disillusioned they would be if you killed yourself."

Maybe we would rebuke him openly, "speaking the truth in love." Tell him to face this behavior as sin, plain and simple. Or maybe we would say, "Elijah, what you need to do is just spend some more time in the Word. Pray, read, meditate."

If we would take any of those approaches with Elijah, we would in effect be saying, "Elijah, you have a spiritual problem. And your spiritual problem is one of two things. It's either a loss of vision or a lack of faith."

In reality, Elijah's depressed condition had nothing to do with his spiritual life. Rather, it was a product of his *social* life. Elijah had spent the last three years in relative solitude, living by a brook in the Kerith Ravine, east of the Jordan River. God fed him miraculously by having ravens drop meat and bread off for him twice a day. He got his water from the brook (until it dried up due to his prayers for drought!). Next, he spent more than two years at a widow's house in the Gentile land of Sidon. While there, God miraculously provided food for him, the woman, and her son, and he miraculously raised the woman's son from the dead.

Elijah apparently stayed at the woman's house till the famine was over. I would guess that he found there a place of quiet retreat. Then one day he received word from God to come back down to the plains of Jezreel—at least a three- or four-day walk from the widow's house in Zarephath. Elijah promptly embarks upon that journey, though very much aware that Ahab's bounty hunters have been searching the area trying to find him for nearly three years!

So, as he talks with Obadiah and then actually encounters King Ahab, Elijah is exhausted from his journey and is undergoing the "culture shock" of coming from a peaceful environment into a hostile, emotionally charged situation.

We read that, "When he [Ahab] saw Elijah, he said to him, 'Is that you, you troubler of Israel?'" (1 Kings 18:17) Ahab is incensed with Elijah because of the famine—the fruit of Elijah's prayer life! This first encounter inaugurates a day of conflict that consummates in a "show-down" of enormous proportions. Elijah challenges the prophets and priests of the god Baal to a public contest on Mount Carmel. The contest concludes with nearly a thousand people being slaughtered at the base of the mountain.

Now we must let our imagination fill in the gaps: The entire contest and outcome on Mount Carmel occupies only about twenty verses in our Bible, yet it is very likely that it lasted from six to ten hours. The false prophets and priests started their ritual prayers early in the day, and by mid-afternoon they hadn't seen or heard a thing from Baal. Can you picture the noise, the confusion, the tension, the conflict and ultimately the screaming and howling as nearly a thousand people are systematically butchered? Can you imagine how traumatic and draining something like this would be? Not to mention the strong possibility that, in the back of Elijah's mind was the nagging question of whether or not Jehovah God *would*, in fact, show himself mighty on Elijah's behalf.

Immediately following this chaotic climax, we are told that Elijah dismissed Ahab and his entourage with a promise of rain, and "climbed to the top of Carmel, bent down to the ground and put his face between his knees" (v. 42). He does this seven times! Finally, when Elijah is convinced that the rain is about to begin, he sends word to Ahab to head back to Jezreel, which was nearly twenty miles away. The Scriptures tell us that, "The power of the LORD came upon Elijah and, tucking his cloak into his belt, he ran ahead of Ahab all the way to Jezreel" (v. 46). Upon reaching Jezreel, he is notified of wicked queen Jezebel's threat to kill him within twenty-four hours. Terrified, Elijah immediately leaves Jezreel and goes to Beersheba in Judah, nearly a one-week journey on foot!

When he arrives at Beersheba, Elijah leaves his servant and goes an additional twenty miles or so into the Judean desert. It is at this point that we pick up the account of a prophet who wants to die.

Why does he want to die? Is it a lack of faith? A loss of vision? I don't think it is either of these. Rather, I think that Elijah is simply "burned out," after two weeks at the center of an emotional and physical whirlwind.

We find in Elijah most of the classic symptoms of burnout—the telltale characteristics of someone whose output has exceeded his resources.

Feelings of Rejection

People who are burned out often believe that no one appreciates them, or perhaps that no one even likes them. Burnout often results from seeing something you've invested all of your time, energy, and resources into simply not materialize. It can be a project at work or church, a relationship, or an idea. I think that Elijah came to believe that, although he had "won" at Carmel, Jezebel was going to have the victory. He had seen enough of the fickle Israelites to know that they would give their allegiance to whomever was in control at the time. He was dealing with the rejection of Jezebel, Ahab, and most likely, the northern kingdom of Israel. Elijah was alone under a broom tree, but I suspect that he came to realize the extent of his loneliness long before he got there.

Isolation

A second symptom of burnout is a desire to be alone. People who are burned out tend to isolate themselves, emotionally or actually, from others. They either build up walls to keep others out of their feelings, or nurture superficial relationships in which the potential for hurt is eliminated and the need to be open and honest is minimized. Look at Elijah. He leaves his servant at Beersheba and walks off into the desert—alone. His sense of isolation can be seen in his conversations with God. Elijah uses the words *I, me,* or *my* ten times in eleven verses! People who are burned out want to be left alone because they are convinced they already *are* alone.

Hopelessness

A third symptom of burnout is the inability to see beyond the present pain, the incapacity to believe that anything can change for the better. Elijah collapses under the broom tree and tells God that life is meaningless and he wants to die. He is convinced that either Jezebel will hunt him down and kill him, or he'll spend the rest of his life as a fugitive, wandering from place to place. He cannot see any chance of recovery or change, much less hope and rest. Elijah's emotional frame of mind is very common among those who are burned out. He can only project the present on into the future. He cannot find any future that is separate from his present experience.

(It is worth noting that nowhere in Elijah's depression did he ever presume upon himself the freedom to fulfill his wishes—to take his own life. He felt the freedom to express his desires, but never assumed the liberty to fulfill them.)

Acute Fatigue

A fourth symptom (or cause!) of burnout is acute physical fatigue, which is always followed or accompanied by emotional weariness. The two are usually inseparable. It is typical and not surprising that almost as soon as Elijah sits down he falls asleep. Can you fault him? Look what he's put his body through in the previous two weeks! People who are burned out are constantly having to reach deep within to find the stamina to complete tasks that were once daily routines. Small challenges suddenly exert enormous demands on the burned out person, often pushing them "over the edge." And most noticeably to others, burned out people are virtually devoid of joy. The message they give to the world is that life is a chore. And tragically, for them it is! They have nothing left to give, even when they want to.

Opinion Becomes Absolute

God appears to our weary prophet, sleeping in a cave (19:9), and asks, "What are you doing here, Elijah?" The prophet pours out his complaint in response:

> "I have been very zealous for the Lord God Almighty. The Israelites have rejected your covenant, broken down your altars, and put your prophets to death with the sword. I am the only one left, and now they are trying to kill me too." (v. 10)

At first glance, Elijah's answer seems reasonable. He believes he is the only faithful servant of God left in all of Israel. His experience of the past couple of months seems to support such a conclusion—until we look at verse 13 of the same chapter: God again appears to Elijah and asks the same question, "What are you doing here, Elijah?" Elijah's response is identical to what he had told the Lord earlier, word for word! One gets the distinct impression that had God asked the weary pilgrim a third time, Elijah would have repeated the same thing.

Elijah's answer was merely the rote recitation of a memorized conclusion about his life. He believed that his own conclusions about life could be trusted absolutely. He assumed that he had all of the information and could make a totally objective evaluation. He didn't see any need for additional input from anyone else. People who are burned out often elevate their own perceptions to the status of truth. How does this happen? In Proverbs 18:1 we read, "He who separates himself seeks his own desire, he quarrels against all sound wisdom" (NASB). When we isolate ourselves from other people, we tend to engage in mental disputes. And the conclusions we draw from these cognitive conflicts are carefully woven into a comprehensive explanation for life.

This is our prophet. His response to God is clearly something he has mentally rehearsed countless times as he walked from Jezreel to Beersheba. He has concluded that he is the only prophet left. And what can one man do against an entire nation? God finally bursts his bubble by telling him, "Yet I reserve seven thousand in Israel—all whose knees have not bowed down to Baal and whose mouths have not kissed him." (1 Kings 19:18)

The prophet Elijah was not a backslider. He was merely a man whose personal expenditures exceeded his resources. A man who burned out. His loss of hope, his desire to be alone, and even the emotional state of mind that prefers death to life, are all symptoms of a life operating on a deficit.

This chapter in Elijah's life should make us more careful about ascribing a spiritual cause for every human shortcoming. If we can't sleep or have chronic headaches, we are often quick to conclude that God has abandoned us or that prayer is ineffectual. We can turn the normal affairs of life in a fallen and sinful world into spiritual battles that crush us further. Elijah stands forever as an example and a warning to us not to quickly prescribe a spiritual cure to a problem that is physical in nature.

But we can best learn from Elijah by determining the actual *cause* of his burnout, and more importantly, by seeing how God dealt with him in that condition.

TWO

Elijah:
The Cause and Cure
of Burnout

We have seen that Elijah's depression was the fruit of fatigue, rather than the outgrowth of a life of unbelief or sin. And his condition is one that exists in abundance among Christians today. Our churches are filled with Christians who are living on the ragged edge of fatigue, disillusioned with fellow Christians and church leaders, perhaps even disappointed with the Christian faith and with God himself. Although there are many attitudes and behaviors that lead to burnout, a few are more common than others.

A Mistaken View of Commitment

One of the prime causes of burnout is a mistaken view of commitment. It is no secret that we live in a success- and results-oriented culture. We are conditioned to look for things to "happen," or more so, to *make* things happen. We talk in terms of profits, results, marketing strategies, and the "bottom line." We believe that real success is always visible and measurable. And more importantly, we believe that success is available to all who are willing to pay the price.

Of course the price of success is total commitment. And total commitment means being as busy as possible, doing as much as you can do, to achieve success. Place this distorted view of commitment into the context of a church or a parachurch organization, and you have all the right ingredients to guarantee that people will either burn out themselves, or cause burnout in the lives they touch.

Commitment to God or to God's work does not mean seeking to accomplish as much as I am able to accomplish before I die. Genuine commitment is simply *doing what God requires of me at the time.* The Scriptures offer numerous examples of people who substituted their own sense of duty for obedience to the specific will of God. Being "busy" for God is not true commitment. In the case of Martha, the sister of Lazarus, her "busy-ness" turned out to be a waste of time. She invested much time and energy preparing a feast for Jesus, only to hear him tell her it would have been better had she spent that time at his feet, listening to him. (Luke 10:38–42)

Commitment to God is simply the willingness to do what he has asked of me. And whenever God asks something of his children, he also provides the strength and grace to accomplish it. Ironically, sometimes commitment to God involves saying no to Christian activities. When our twin girls were born, I had to decline numerous opportunities to speak and minister to others because I believed God had called me to minister to my wife and four children. Such missed opportunities can become a source of great guilt for Christians if they don't understand that being committed to God means doing what *he* requires, no matter what others say or think. Being committed to God means that I get my job assignments from him, not from others or even from myself. When I become enmeshed in a life of activity that does not have God's sanction I will burn out, because I am seeking to accomplish that for which God has given me neither the strength nor the grace. When I embark on such a course, it will only be a matter of time before I collapse—emotionally, spiritually, or physically. One famous missionary who died very young made this statement shortly before he died: "God gave me a horse to ride and a message to proclaim. I have killed the horse and can no longer carry the message."

Total commitment has less to do with intensity than it does with duration. The question is not, What have you accomplished for God? but rather, Will you still be walking with God at the end of your life? The apostle Paul, facing execution at the hands of the Romans, said, "I have fought the good fight, I have finished the race, I have kept the faith" (2 Tim. 4:7). It is significant that Paul didn't boast how many "rounds" he went in the fight, how many "knockouts" he tallied, or how many foes he vanquished. He also didn't allude to his "speed" in the race or how far he ran. In fact, Paul didn't even suggest that he had "won" the race. Rather, Paul was grateful to God, as his life drew to a close, that he had *finished* the race. Commitment to God means that we have a passion to finish, more than to achieve. It has to do with duration, not intensity or success. Any view of commitment to God that emphasizes results over obedience and intensity over endurance has its origin in the mind of man, not the heart of God. And it is a prime cause of burnout.

A Mistaken View of Responsibility

Although we would seldom admit it, sometimes we come to believe that God cannot fulfill his plans without us. If we don't keep busy, God will be left helplessly in the lurch. While it is true that God has entrusted the work of ministry to human beings, our role in God's plan must be understood against the larger backdrop of just who our God is. As he debated the Greek philosophers of Athens, Paul proclaimed,

> "The God who made the world and everything in it is the Lord of heaven and earth and does not live in temples built by hands. And he is not served by human hands, as if he needed anything, because he himself gives all men life and breath and everything else." (Acts 17:24–25)

God does not "need" us. He can easily get along without us. We are not indispensable to him. If you, or I, or even the most influential Christian alive were to die tonight, God would not have to rewrite his plan for human history. This is an important truth to apprehend, because it is all too easy to develop the attitude that, if I don't do such-and-such, it simply won't get done!

If God has not called us to do something, he will not provide the grace and strength to do it. And if those vital elements are absent, we will eventually burn out no matter how sincere we are. Sadly, there are believers scattered throughout every city and town in this country who have been burned out in church work, community projects, and school committees. Even the relatively recent obsession among young parents that their children must be exposed to every opportunity available by the time they are in junior high, is a powerful contributor to the quiet assassination of our strength, resources, and hope. This is particularly true of young mothers who feel compelled to "stimulate" their toddler through programs, sports, and a plethora of extra activities that take them outside the home and into the car. Yet in conversation with these burned-out moms, you'll quickly get the message that all of this activity is "necessary" for the proper development of their children.

My primary responsibility is to God, not to society or even the church. My role as a Christian and my responsibilities as a father, mother, or employee must all fall under the umbrella of my ultimate responsibility to God. This does not mean, of course, that I am to be insubordinate on the job, selfish with my time, or disinterested in the needs of those around me. It simply means that my priorities must coincide with what God desires, and that my energies are spent doing what he demands. Anything that is done for eternity is accomplished only by God touching human efforts with his own endowment, never because of the degree of our strain or the cleverness of our methods.

Understanding the principle of God's independence is vital for helping us determine what is worthwhile and what is not. But it is also necessary to fully grasp this principle in order to say no to those who will allow or actually induce burnout in others. Too often in Christian circles gifted, willing, and effective people are simply used by others. And this is as true of organizations like the church as it is of individual Christians. It is no secret that 90 percent of the work done in churches is done by 10 percent of the membership. The current exhortation to "just say no" applies to church-activity addiction as well as to any other addiction. We are of little lasting value to God, ourselves, and the world, if we don't "finish the race," faithful to him. And this can only be accomplished if we have a biblical understanding of God's independence and its corollary, a proper view of our own responsibility to him and his purposes.

It is very likely that Elijah fell prey to this debilitating misunderstanding. His statement that, "I am the only one left" is more likely a cry of exasperation in the face of overwhelming feelings of responsibility, than a proclamation of his own fidelity. He had assumed too much responsibility. He had forgotten that God, not man, changes hearts and controls human history. And Elijah faltered under such a load, just as we so often do.

A Poorly Ordered Inner Life

Gordon MacDonald, in his excellent book, *Ordering Your Private World*[3] differentiates between a "driven" person and a "called" person. Driven people are perfect examples of the type of lifestyle discussed above—a distorted view of commitment and an inflated sense of responsibility. Driven people's entire existence is fueled

---

[3]Gordon MacDonald, *Ordering Your Private World* (Nashville: Nelson, 1985).

by what "ought" to be done, and their sense of worth is determined by their performance—and by other people's opinions about that performance.

MacDonald cites King Saul as an example of a driven person, and John the Baptist as one who was called. Saul's life was characterized by a constant attempt to please others. In fact at one of the low points of his life, he confessed to Samuel that the reason he had disobeyed God was because he "was afraid of the people [his own soldiers!] and so I gave in to them." (1 Sam. 15:24)

John the Baptist, on the other hand, never lost sight of his *calling*, which was to prepare the world for Jesus Christ. Though well-known as the first prophet to Israel in 400 years, he was willing to exchange his fame for obscurity. In fact, when John was told that he was actually *losing* followers to Jesus, he responded, "He must become greater; I must become less." (John 3:30)

How does one account for the stark contrast between Saul and John? John the Baptist, says MacDonald, had a well-ordered private world. He had spent years in the Judean countryside praying, fasting, and meditating in preparation for the coming of Jesus. He had gotten his direction from God, not from the crowds or the circumstances. Because John's inner world was keen and strong, he didn't panic when he began to lose followers. John knew clearly what he was supposed to be about, and therefore he did not fall into what MacDonald says are the two most common snares for people with weak inner worlds.

First, says MacDonald, those who do not take the time to cultivate a strong private world—the disciplines of personal piety—will spend all of their time and energy nurturing their *outer* world, the world of people and activities. When we do this, out of necessity we will arrange our lives to satisfy the demands, expectations, and opinions of others rather than seeking to please God. And because peoples' demands on us will always exceed our resources, if we order our lives around our outer worlds we will eventually burn out, break down, or both. Elijah was more concerned about what Jezebel and the people of Israel thought of him than about God's opinion. And that misplaced concern eventually took its toll.

A second trap driven people fall into, says MacDonald, is that they will tend to accumulate power. This is especially true of those in positions of leadership and notoriety. But power tends to corrupt those who wield it, because they focus all their attention on their outer worlds to the neglect of the inner. King Saul was an eloquent speaker and an excellent military commander. But he had virtually no support from his inner world. Over time, he began to listen to what others were saying about him more than what God was telling him to do. Saul was broad and shallow rather than focused and deep.

Saul's inverted life eventually toppled, as all such lives do. And the higher one is in the eyes of others, the greater the distance to the bottom. We have seen these principles illustrated for us time and time again in recent years with the downfall of politicians, tel-evangelists, and other church leaders.

Our inner worlds are fed and nourished by regular times of prayer and Bible reading. These activities need to be as important to us as eating and sleeping. Driven people often neglect both their spiritual and their bodily needs. And when the outer world of activities and recognition begins to make demands that their inner world of character and substance cannot meet, they either crash or burn out.

Misunderstanding of Ourselves

A fourth contributor to burnout has to do with our lack of understanding of our own individuality—the unique way that God has made each of us and how that affects what he expects of us. Too often, we base our behavior on mental images of what Christians are *supposed* to be and do. But the Scriptures repeatedly inform us that God has made each of us unique and has gifted us in specific ways. "For by the grace given me I say to everyone of you: Do not think of yourselves more highly than you ought, but rather think of yourself with sober judgment, in accordance with the measure of faith God has given you" (Rom. 12:3). Paul repeats this principle in 2 Corinthians 8:12: "For if the willingness is there, the gift is acceptable according to what one has, not according to what he does not have." Even though the context here is the giving of our finances, the principle is the same: God expects us to give out of what we have (and are) not out of what we don't have (and are not).

This is especially important in regard to our time and energies, not to mention our emotions. God has given each Christian a supernatural endowment—a spiritual gift—with which to serve him (1 Cor. 12:4–7). One of the most certain ways to guarantee burnout is to continually engage in an activity for which we are not gifted. Those in leadership can do the same type of damage by demanding that those in their organization assume responsibilities or perform activities which are beyond their giftedness and therefore outside the normal flow of God's strength and grace.

I am convinced that God has given me the spiritual gift of teaching, and Jill the gift of encouragement. The fastest way to burn us out, or for us to burn ourselves out, is to reverse those responsibilities for a prolonged period of time. I am terrible at long-term loyalty in ministering to people; Jill chafes under the rigors of preparing lessons and the emotional drain of having to perform in front of people. It is not ungodly for either of us to decline involvement and responsibility that takes us beyond our giftedness for prolonged periods of time. We've tried it, and the cost to us emotionally, spiritually, and physically was enormous.

God tells us our "performance" is acceptable if it issues out of what we *have*, and what we have is what he has specifically given us. Seeking to function in a manner that is inconsistent with the way God has gifted us is the surest road to burnout or breakdown.

A second route is to deny the way God has individually equipped us to relate to others.

Extroverts and Introverts

God in his wisdom made each of us unique. As Christians we have elevated this notion nearly to the status of a doctrine. But even though we proclaim it in our theology, we tend to ignore or deny it in our practice. It is more common for us to expect others to be *like* us than it is for us to "celebrate" the fact that they are different. We are put off if someone can't handle things that we can, or prefers to do things differently from us. Comments like, "I don't know why she's so overwhelmed with three children. I've got four and I'm doing fine!" Or, "Why are you so disorganized? You create more work for yourself than you realize!" While we verbally affirm that our uniqueness is evidence of God's infinite creativity, we deny its reality when we measure others by our own standards. We elevate our own preferences to the category of "shoulds" and "oughts" for those around us. And in so doing, we negate anything else we may have said about the beauty of human uniqueness.

One of the ways the Lord saw fit to distinguish us from one another has to do with which "world" we prefer to live in. Some of us have been made to function best in the inner world of ideas and possibilities. Others prefer the outer world of people and things. These two types of people have been christened "introverts" and "extroverts."

A great deal of misunderstanding surrounds these two labels. In America, introversion is nearly considered a disease, or at least a liability. Introverts are thought of as closet-dwellers, people who prefer books to people, and who cringe if drawn out of isolation.

Extroverts, on the other hand, are perceived as the "life of the party," the movers and shakers of the world. They are the "go-getter" types that every committee thinks they need to get their work done. Extroverts are often marked as people-lovers, while introverts arouse the suspicion that they dislike their fellow humans. Nothing could be further from the truth.

The primary difference between extroverts and introverts has to do with where their primary stimulation comes from. It has little or nothing to do with their affinity to others. Introverts are stimulated from *within*, extroverts from *without*. Both enjoy people. Both need people. But being with people, particularly groups of people, is costly to an introvert. The stimulation from social encounters provokes deep reflection and inner processing of what was said and what happened during the encounter. An introvert takes a social encounter with them when they leave. Extroverts, on the other hand, are stimulated by the social processes. They are actually motivated and energized simply by being around people. But, when these external stimuli are no longer present, the extrovert either attaches himself to the next stimulating environment, or begins to become lethargic.

Jill is an introvert, I am an extrovert. When we go over to someone's house for dinner, I am at my best. I love to talk (especially about myself!) and interact. It is not uncommon for me to occupy center stage on such occasions. Jill, on the other hand, will connect with one or two people, slip off into a corner, and spend the evening engaged in a deeply stimulating conversation. Both of us are with people, and both of us enjoy it. But when we leave to go home, I leave the dinner party behind. Jill takes it home with her. She will lie awake in bed thinking about a person's marriage problems, or something they said or did. Meanwhile, stimulation absent, I am sound asleep!

The reason this is so vital is that our culture tends to idolize and promote extroverted role models. Even within Christian circles, we are mesmerized by "dynamic speakers," "motivating seminars," and the cult of celebrity. By contrast, introverts appear dull and boring, perhaps even inferior to their sparky counterparts. Being outgoing, positive, even loud or obnoxious, is falsely equated with being an "exciting" Christian who is filled with "the joy of the Lord." The more quiet, introverted Christian is perceived as defeated or second-class.

This is a tremendous tragedy. For one thing, introverts are the real geniuses in the world. You would be very hard-pressed to find an extroverted inventor, novelist, artist, or songwriter. We extroverts simply do not have the ability to focus and persist that is so essential to genuine creative work. Extroverts tend to get all the credit for introverts' ideas.

We can burn ourselves out—or worse, burn *others* out—by neglecting to acknowledge this significant difference in our basic design. To ask introverts to assume responsibilities best suited to extroverts is a quick way to crush them. To ask extroverts to continually perform tasks that demand focus, extended time alone, or prolonged quiet is to deny the way God made them.

This of course is not to say that given individuals *cannot* function in certain roles. We must be open to do whatever the Lord asks of us. But to deny that the Lord has so constructed our temperaments and personalities that we function best in certain environments and tasks, is short-sighted, and in the long run, can ruin ourselves and others.

Because we have four children, Jill is already pretty "maxed-out" each day just with the daily responsibilities of being a wife and mother. To ask her to head up a church nursery or a children's program would be tantamount to slow suffocation. It is unfortunate when we saddle people with guilt because they decline taking on one more responsibility. It is not a sin to say no to something if I know I cannot function in that capacity—although it certainly may be a sin to say no to something simply because I don't feel like doing it. The difference is real, even if those we have to submit our refusal to can't see it. Maturity demands that we recognize that God has made us to function best in different roles and environments.

There is, of course, another side to this discussion: The Bible makes it clear that God can use our *weaknesses* to glorify him (see 2 Cor. 4:1–15, 12:7–10). We all are aware of instances in our lives in which God accomplished something of significance in spite of, or even perhaps because of, a weakness. We should never use our introversion or extroversion as an excuse for disobedience.

Yet the larger principle still stands: It is unusual for God to expect us to function for a prolonged period of time in a capacity for which he has not shaped us.

We can minimize, perhaps even eliminate some burnout in our lives and the lives of others by recognizing that God has not only gifted us for certain tasks, but that he has also constructed us to function best in certain environments. Failing to recognize the seriousness of these human and spiritual distinctives is to court disaster.

A fifth contributor to burnout has to do with our inability or unwillingness to relax.

Working at Our Play

Gordon Dahl has said, "Most middle-class Americans tend to worship their work, to work at their play, and to play at their worship. As a result, their meanings and values are distorted. Their relationships disintegrate faster than they can keep them in repair, and their life-styles resemble a cast of characters in search of a plot."[4] Dahl concludes that most Americans are lacking a mean-

---

[4]Gordon Dahl, *Work, Play, and Worship in a Leisure-Oriented Society* (Minneapolis: Augsburg, 1972), 12.

ingful life because of these jumbled priorities. The three areas he spotlights—work, play, and worship—are all vital, and each makes its unique contribution to burnout. A number of authors have addressed the problems associated with "Type A" personalities, workaholics, and those striving to climb the corporate ladder. A multitude of books have also been written assessing the plight of the church and its need for renewal and revival. But few have addressed the topic of *play*, or relaxation. It is this aspect of Dahl's statement that I wish to examine.

Dahl says that Americans "work at their play." We simply do not know how to relax. A brief tour of any of the parks in your area will affirm the validity of Dahl's perception. Take an afternoon (if you have a free one!) and visit a local park. Watch the "recreational" softball, soccer, or basketball matches that are going on. Or better yet, visit a health and fitness spa and look for enjoyment on the faces of those who are snorting and perspiring in front of mirrors, or the near masochistic maneuvers of those engaging in "high-impact" aerobics.

These are all excellent indicators that we "work" at our play. But the classic illustration is the American runner: Clothed in neon spandex outfits that you'd swear run on batteries, headsets strapped to their waists, these emperors of exercise are as serious as a heart attack about their running. The purpose? The *stated* purpose is to maintain a healthy cardiovascular system—to stay in shape. But their real purpose seems to be simply to "work out," with the emphasis on *work*. Runners don't run for enjoyment. They run with two goals in mind: increasing their distance; or decreasing their time. And they work hard at it.

Americans simply don't seem to know how to relax. And rather than rethinking our recreational philosophy, we've created an entire industry that *enables* us to work at our play. The title of Tim Hansel's book, *When I Relax, I Feel Guilty*, could easily be stamped on our coins in place of "In God We Trust"!

This inability to relax is not confined to the world of parks, spas, and tracks. It has invaded the world of pulpits, pews, and potlucks. We as Christians are as guilty as, perhaps even more guilty than the larger culture. In our lifestyle (though perhaps not in our theology) we have unconsciously relegated relaxation to the realm of "sin." We would deny it, but it's true. Unless we believe something positive will emerge from relaxation, we feel guilty about doing it. We don't read Christian books as enjoyment. We have to *learn* something that will help us be better parents, spouses, neighbors, or servants of God. We don't even read our Bibles because we enjoy it. Many of us feel this pressure to read so many chapters each day so that we can put a little check on our "Reading Program," or move on to the next section of our "One-Year Bible." Unless we are convinced that some measurable good will come from relaxation, we are hesitant, even unwilling to do it. And this twisted understanding of rest contributes to burnout too.

Jesus made a powerful statement regarding rest in Mark 2:27: "The Sabbath was made for man, not man for the Sabbath." I was raised as a Roman Catholic, and being in church on Sunday was no option. I grew up with a very legalistic understanding of the Sabbath. It was a day of duty and obligation. Jesus' statement refutes that idea. He actually says that God had *us* in mind when he instituted the Sabbath. Even the title, "The Lord's Day," though biblical and accurate, tends to draw us away from the idea that there is something in the Sabbath for *us.*

Could it be that we are missing one of the greatest blessings God has provided for us—namely, that the Sabbath was instituted for us, to provide a day of needed rest? Isaiah tells us that God wants us to reserve the Sabbath for him, to refrain from our own activities and to meditate on him and his works. And if we do those things, he promises that we will be refreshed (Isa. 58:13–14). Sadly, the Sabbath is frequently a Christian's busiest day! Typically, we rush off to Sunday school and church in the morning; perhaps a meeting or choir practice right after dinner; and then evening service. Then, with Monday's dawn, the race starts all over again.

For many of us, Sunday has become a day of non-stop religious activity rather than of rest. There is no place in the Bible where God has said that the Sabbath was supposed to be a day devoted totally to public worship. The message of God in Scripture is that the Sabbath is to be a day of private rest. We of all people have an opportunity to rest and relax. Yet, we don't do so any more than the larger culture. And like our secular twins, we lead lives characterized by fatigue and discouragement, the symptoms of burnout.

Prescriptions for Recovery

Fortunately, burnout is not terminal. It is remediable, but often not without radical change fueled by rigid determination. One of the quickest things we can do is to examine our schedules. Assuming that we are burned out or depressed, and we think that exhaustion is the likely culprit, taking a quick personal inventory of the thieves of time and energy in our lives can be revealing. Sit down with a calendar and take a look at your schedule for the next month. Simply looking at what you are *doing* each day can be an excellent way to determine whether your depression is logistical or spiritual in origin.

The main reason this chapter is in the beginning of the study is that many Christians attribute spiritual causes to everything. And the most paralyzing and painful thing that I have discovered in my own life, is to attribute a spiritual cause to something that doesn't have one. It forces me to spend all of my time and energies looking for an answer which doesn't exist. Not only is it a huge waste of time, it actually compounds the problem by eroding my diminishing strength even further, as well as creating an imaginary spiritual issue that quickly becomes a weapon Satan can use against me. Elijah was convinced he had a spiritual problem. But God did not provide him with a spiritual answer. At least not right away.

Look at your schedule. What does it tell you? How many nights a week are you away from home? I refuse to be away from home at night. It's a conviction I have. Not all men can do that; but many Christians could easily be out at night and away from home less than they are.

Another, closely related step we can take is to eliminate useless activities. Are there things we are doing that are of no consequence to ourselves, God, or anyone else? Have we created "machinery" in our lives that has no purpose other than to keep itself going? Something that has no benefit of any kind, but because it "needs to be done" we do it?

When I worked as a chemist, my immediate supervisor nearly burned out me and the other two chemists, generating data. Data, data, data! Finally, one day I asked him, "What do you do with the data from this test we do for you each day?"

"Oh, nothing really. We need to measure that and keep a handle on it," was his reply.

I said, "Well, what for? You're not using it for anything." In the course of that conversation I discovered to my dismay that four or five of the analyses we were doing each week, amounting to about ten hours worth of labor, were merely taking up space in his file cabinet. And very honestly I said, "I don't think we should continue to do this. I can't continue to ask my staff to do this." Thankfully he came around to seeing it that way too.

Even away from the work place, in our own lives, we can frequently do things just for the sake of doing them. Churches are notorious for this. "We've always done it this way." "We've always had a midweek service." No one comes, no one benefits, but the machinery churns on. Sometimes we just need to eliminate things.

Of course we need to be careful that we don't eliminate things we truly need, like sleep. How much time are you spending in bed?

Are you rising early and going to bed late? God warns us in Psalm 127:2, "It is vain to rise up early and go late to rest, eating the bread of anxious toil; for he gives to his beloved sleep" (RSV). My version of this verse is, "If you burn the candle at both ends, you'll eventually run out of wax." God wants us to take time, perhaps even *make* time, to sleep. This is illustrated beautifully in the way he dealt with Elijah.

Elijah essentially said, "O Lord, beam me up! It's all over. I can't take it any more!" Then he lay down and fell asleep! Then, an angel came along, tapped him on the shoulder, and fed him a good meal. Then, he fell asleep a second time! Why? He was exhausted! We would have been too. Perhaps we already are. For some of us when we're depressed, the best thing we can do is close our Bible, put off our introspection, put on our pajamas, and go to bed. It is very significant that Elijah slept *twice* before God ever attempted to talk to him. We usually try to reverse that process and demand that God speak to us in our hour of exhaustion rather than after it.

If you are working long and sleeping short, and you are depressed, chances are three or four nights of eight to ten hours of sleep will bring you to a place where things seem more manageable and less terminal. If your present living conditions will not allow you to recapture your lost rest, find a place that will. Invest the money, if need be, and check into a motel for two or three days; or find a friend who will be out of town for a while and will let you stay at his or her house. If you determine that your depression is the product of insufficient rest, do whatever you need to do, to get some rest.

Are We What We Eat?

The American fitness industry has a gold mine on its hands. Most of its clientele arrive sometime after 5 P.M. to begin working at their play. After an hour or so of high-impact aerobics, their bodies pulsating in a perspirated frenzy, they shower and exit, feeling good about themselves and their bodies. For many, the next stop is "Happy Hour" at a favorite night spot, to meet with friends who have just left their own favorite fitness center, also feeling great. After a few drinks, a lot of empty talk and promises to see each other tomorrow, they all go home . . . to eat dinner! Because most of what we eat after five o'clock turns to fat, tomorrow's workout is actually a work-*off* of last night's meal! And so goes the lifestyle of the man who works at his play.

For many of us, diet can be a significant contributor to our emotional frame of mind. A high-carbohydrate, low-protein diet can become an assassin for those who are running the burnout track. One diet specialist has said that we should eat breakfast like a king, lunch like a prince, and dinner like a pauper. Unfortunately, most of us have those suggestions reversed. We either skip breakfast altogether or grab a donut and cup of coffee on our way to work; have another sugar-and-caffeine fix at mid-morning; something fried and fast for lunch; and we top it off with a large and late dinner to inaugurate the final stage of our daily routine—relative inactivity.

Proper rest, a balanced diet, and adequate exercise (at the proper times), are essential. The unity of body and spirit is evidenced for us in the life of Elijah. Before God addressed Elijah's problem, he saw to it that the prophet had two good periods of sleep and two meals. God *fed* Elijah before he fellowshipped with him. He saw to it that Elijah got adequate *rest* before he gave him revelation. That order of things is more than interesting or coincidental. Our bodily needs, when unmet, can poison our spiritual sensibilities and perceptions. That is exactly what had happened to the prophet Elijah.

Cultivating a Strong Private World

A third way to defuse the depression caused by fatigue is to examine our private world, that inner citadel of our spiritual life. Am I feeding daily on God's Word? Am I taking time each day to dig out spiritual food for myself? This is drastically different from a devotional or Bible-reading "program." It is cultivating a relationship with God himself. MacDonald, in *Ordering Your Private World* warns that, if we don't seek to cultivate such a relationship, "we will never learn to enjoy the eternal and infinite perspective on reality that we were created to have."[5] That's what had happened to Elijah. He had come to believe everything was hopeless. "Take me home, Lord. I'm the only prophet left." He totally lost sight of who God was, that he was in control, and that he could be trusted. MacDonald says that the only way to maintain a proper, eternal perspective, is by spending time in God's Word. It seems to be a principle that when we slack off on our time with God in the Scriptures, our entire perspective starts to cloud over—much like a window that slowly gets smudged with fingerprints.

This, says MacDonald, is compounded by the fact that our most important needs do not immediately alert us when they are neglected.[6] My need for a strong inner world, my need for a genuine time of rest and refreshment, my need to laugh—these things that are so crucial will not sound an alarm or wave a red flag when I neglect them. If I let a week go by without meeting with God, I won't come home one day to find an angel in my room who says, "Fran, we need to talk."

What happens if we don't show up at work for four days? Or skip all our meals for a week? We have nearly instant feedback that that area of our life is out of order. But this simply doesn't happen with our inner world. Our most important needs, those of

---

[5]MacDonald, *Ordering Your Private World*, 119.
[6]MacDonald, *Ordering Your Private World*, 84.

our inner world, don't alert us when we neglect them. It would be nice if they did, but they simply don't. We may see the *consequences* of that neglect in our relationships, but we aren't immediately aware of the cause.

Ordering our inner world simply means we make sure that there are no encroachments upon it. That there's a section of our life which no one can take away from us. If we do that, says MacDonald, we will be creating a place where God can visit and where he can speak personally and regularly.

Once we have established this regular time with God, we need to be on guard lest it become routine, just one more mindless behavior on our daily treadmill. We need to be creative in our devotional life. When I first became a Christian, I used to take a casual walk early each morning, talking openly and aloud to God. It was marvelous. I walked alongside a babbling brook, and reviewed the memory verses I was working on at the time. One day I would read from a hymnal, another day perhaps listen to a tape, or even play my guitar and sing to God.

But then that all changed. One day I met an older Christian who told me that my routine was all wrong. He said, "If you want to have a 'quiet time,' you should get a cup of tea or coffee, sit at your desk with a pen and paper, and seriously study God's Word."

I did that for a couple of years. But I really lost something in the process. When I recently went for a walk one day, and talked things through with God just like I used to do, the joy returned. A wise servant of God once told me, "Brother, a devotional life is not some program. A devotional life is a life devoted to God."

So be creative. Don't get stuck in a rut where the procedure becomes an end in itself. Play a piano, sing, go for a walk. Do whatever you need to do to keep you devotional life alive and meaningful. But above all, create a place where God can visit and speak.

A fourth way to defuse the depression is a big one on my list. If I could tattoo two words on the foreheads of Christians in America it would be, "Lighten up!" We seem to be serious about all the wrong things. We take ourselves so seriously, but we're not really serious about the Lord. If more Christians had a sense of humor, I think it would work miracles in regard to depression. An important way to avoid burnout it to learn to live comfortably with who we are. And the only way that can happen is to have a sense of humor. Otherwise we are constantly making unrealistic demands on ourselves, or inflating events and mistakes to a level of importance they simply don't deserve. Life is full of failures, but failure is manageable if I know how to laugh. We have a poster in our kitchen of Garfield and Odie throwing pies at each other. The caption says, "We must all learn to laugh at ourselves." That poster has saved our family from many an unwarranted conflict by forcing us to lighten up.

Are you exposing yourself to *opportunities* for laughter? When journalist Norman Cousins discovered he had a terminal illness, he decided he would try to heal it with laughter. He gathered together some old slapstick movies, such as the Marx Brothers and the Three Stooges, and watched them for two hours each day. The laughter brought about changes in his body chemistry, and he was healed! He wrote a book about it, titled *The Anatomy of an Illness*.[7] There are studies being done on the curative power of laughter. But that laughter can heal should come as no surprise to a student of the Bible. In Proverbs 17:20 we read, "A cheerful heart is good medicine, but a downcast spirit dries up the bones." Humor has a good physiological effect on the human body. Are you allowing yourself opportunities to laugh?

Another way to combat depression is to avoid chronic isolation. One of Elijah's biggest mistakes was isolating himself from the counsel of his friends. In his prolonged time alone, Elijah concluded that he was the only faithful Jew left in all of Israel! This

---

[7]Norman Cousins, *The Anatomy of an Illness as Perceived by the Patient* (New York: Norton, 1979).

conclusion was totally wrong. Yet because Elijah had no one to talk to, he came to believe that his ideas were reality. Isolation tends to convince us of things that aren't true. We need to make sure that we are not cutting ourselves off from others.

Satan knows the vulnerability of isolated Christians. Peter tells us that Satan prowls around like a roaring lion, seeking someone to devour, and one of the classic hunting tactics of lions is to isolate their prey from the rest of the herd. Once this is accomplished, the lion has an easy kill. This is equally true of people.

Isolation can be especially problematic for mothers of young children. Being with small children all day, every day, is a form of isolation. It is isolation from the stimulation provided by adult peers. Husbands need to enable their wives to spend at least one day a week—preferably two—away from home. Jill went to a "Mom's Morning Out" program two or three mornings a week when our twins were toddlers. It helped her cope with the threat of depression from both isolation and exhaustion.

A final suggestion for dealing with the discouragement that comes from fatigue, is to take time for yourself. By "taking time" I don't merely mean doing something fun once in a while. Rather, I mean to literally "take" time. Mark it down on the calendar, set an appointment to meet with yourself. If we are not aggressive in allocating time for ourselves, it will be quickly hijacked by the powerful people in our lives—those whom we feel we must please, or whose praise we have learned to enjoy. We should set aside time for ourselves well in advance, and then guard it tenaciously. Of course there are times when we will have to sacrifice our personal time for genuine, immediate demands. But that must be the exception, never the rule. Most of the things that want to take these times from us are not necessary. The urgent is often the greatest enemy of the best.

Elijah was convinced that he was trapped in a helpless spiritual dilemma. But the truth was that he was physically and emotionally burned out. If he had persisted in believing his problem was spiritual in nature rather than physical, he would never have found any lasting solutions. He would only have driven himself further into depression. Some depression can be best dealt with by sleep, relaxation, laughter, and time for ourselves, rather than by hours of therapy and introspection.

THREE

Moses: Unwillingness to Delegate Responsibility

Moses, along with David and Abraham, is one of the three key people in the history of the Jews. As we look at the life of Moses, we're going to consider a type of depression that resulted from his failure to learn something God tried to teach him. It is a type of depression that affects men in their jobs, women in their homes, and anyone who is in a position of management or authority.

As our story opens, in Numbers 11:4–6, we read, "The rabble with them began to crave other food, and again the Israelites started wailing and said, 'If only we had meat to eat! We remember the fish we ate in Egypt at no cost—also the cucumbers, melons, leeks, onions and garlic. But now we have lost our appetite; we never see anything but this manna!'"

The people are issuing an enormous complaint about God's provision. And the complaint is directed toward the one God had appointed to lead them—Moses. We are later told that, "Moses heard the people of every family wailing, each at the entrance to his tent. The LORD became exceedingly angry, and Moses was troubled. He asked the LORD, 'Why have you brought this trouble on your servant?'" (vv. 10–11) Moses turns the whole thing back to God, asking why God was doing this to him. "What have I done to displease you that you put the burden of all these people on me?

Did I conceive all these people? Did I give them birth? Why do you tell me to carry them in my arms, as a nurse carries an infant, to the land you promised on oath to their forefathers? Where can I get meat for all these people? They keep wailing to me, 'Give us meat to eat!' I cannot carry all these people by myself; the burden is too heavy for me. If this is how you are going to treat me, put me to death right now—if I have found favor in your eyes—and do not let me face my own ruin.'" (vv. 11–15)

It would seem rather likely that Moses is depressed! He is obviously angry; but he is also depressed—enough so that he wants to die! It is interesting that Moses refers to himself sixteen times in only five verses. As we have seen, focusing on self to the exclusion of others is a common behavior among those who are depressed. Moses cannot see beyond his mirror. He is throwing a "pity party," and hoping that God will come to his party.

Before trying to understand the actual cause of Moses' depression, we need to review his life up to this point. It will be helpful to see what he has *already* gone through with the people of Israel.

The event under consideration occurs approximately one year after the Exodus from Egypt. God has been providing manna for Israel since shortly after they left the security of their bondage. Now they are very agitated about their "accommodations" in the wilderness, and they are quick to verbalize their dissatisfaction to Moses. Perhaps they had thought that the "land flowing with milk and honey" was going to be a beautiful retreat center. They had quickly forgotten the conditions of bondage they had left behind in Egypt, and were totally focused on the difficulties of the present. Numbers 11:10 tells us that the "people of every family" were wailing at the entrance to their tents. Verse 21 reveals that there were 600,000 men alone. Using a conservative estimate, we can guess that there were at least one-and-a-half-million people "wailing at the entrance to their tents"! Can you imagine this? Can you picture the noise and confusion? Then consider that every person in this multitude is upset with the same person—Moses.

And he's depressed.

Wouldn't you be! It would be like working the Customer Service line at a department store the day after Christmas . . . when everyone in town comes to return merchandise. Moses is facing a veritable sea of wailing, shouting, complaining people. Can't you just imagine what they are saying to him as he walks past their tents? "Great job, Moses!" "Hey, thanks a bunch!"

Moses wants God to kill him right on the spot: "If this is how you are going to treat me, put me to death right now" (v. 15). Moses is basically telling God that this whole thing was *his* idea. *He* was the one who wanted to "deliver" Israel. He was the one who brought them out into the wilderness. He was the one they were really mad at—it's just that, conveniently, God is not visible, so Moses has become their target.

Moses has had it. He wants out, and he wants out now! He realizes that he can no longer carry this multitude alone, so he tells God to end his agony, quickly.

Moses is surely being quite honest concerning his own emotional condition. He is depressed, angry, frustrated, and really does want "out" of the arrangement. But he is wrong about the solution.

Have you ever been in a situation in your home, job, or church, where you were absolutely overwhelmed with responsibility? There's too much to do, too little time, not enough resources. And you just want out! You want to quit, or run away, or both. That is exactly where Moses is in this passage. His "solution," his way of "quitting," is to die. Death is always the easy way out. But Moses is missing something God has been trying to teach him.

Good Advice From a Father-in-law

In order to understand what God has been trying to teach Moses, we need to turn back to Exodus 18, when the Jews had been out of Egypt for only a short while (19:1 states that it has been three months since the Exodus). Although we cannot be certain exactly when chapter 18 occurs, we know that their Red Sea experience is still very vivid in their minds. They are still "wet behind the ears" in regard to their new relationship with God through Moses. So far, they have witnessed the miraculous parting of the Red Sea, the supernatural purification of the waters of Mara, the supernatural daily provision of manna, and water coming from a rock to quench their thirst. These miracles are all part of their "national resumé."

In chapter 18 Moses' father-in-law, Jethro, comes to visit him. Moses comes out to meet him (v. 7), bows down in respect, and welcomes him. The two of them go into Moses' tent and Moses recounts to his father-in-law all the amazing things God has done since he and his people left Egypt. You get the picture of a son-in-law trying to convince his wife's father that everything is going great. He's enjoying his "work," and has been very successful at what he's doing. Jethro, it seems, shares Moses' enthusiasm and joy.

The next day Moses "goes to work" and Jethro accompanies him, perhaps to catch a glimpse of his son-in-law in action. The account of what happens that day is very revealing and has tremendous relevance to what happens to Moses in Numbers 11:

> The next day Moses took his seat to serve as judge for the people, and they stood around him from morning till evening. When his father-in-law saw all that Moses was doing for the people, he said, "What is this you are doing for the people? Why do you alone sit as judge, while all these people stand around you from morning till evening?" (Ex. 18:13–14)

Moses responds in a fairly standard and predictable way: "Because the people come to me to seek God's will. Whenever they have a dispute, it is brought to me, and I decide between the parties and inform them of God's decrees and laws" (v. 15). In other words, "Well, Dad, it's my job! I'm the mediator. I'm the deliverer. God has always used me to mediate between the people and himself. What do you mean, 'Why do I do these things?'"

Moses also clearly implies that the people *need* him to do these things. Someone has to do them, and Moses is the one best suited for the role. After all, wasn't he the one who got the tablets from God in the first place? Wasn't he the one who heard, directly from God, all of the Law that he's supposed to use to arbitrate their disputes? Isn't it logical that he should be the one doing the judging? Who else could possibly do it?

Jethro tells his son-in-law that this method is not wise: "Moses' father-in-law replied, 'What you are doing is not good. You and these people who come to you will only wear yourselves out. The work is too heavy for you; you cannot handle it alone'" (18:17–18). Jethro tells Moses that what he's *doing* is great, but how he's going about it is not. As an outsider, Jethro is in an excellent position to objectively assess Moses' daily routine and make suggestions. And Jethro has only one suggestion—delegate responsibility:

> Listen now to me and I will give you some advice, and may God be with you. You must be the people's representative before God and bring their disputes to him. Teach them the decrees and laws, and show them the way to live and the duties they are to perform. But select capable men from all the people—men who fear God, trustworthy men who hate dishonest gain—and appoint them as officials over thousands, hundreds, fifties and tens. Have them serve as judges for the people at all times, but have them bring every difficult case to you; the simple cases they can decide themselves. That will make your load lighter, because they will share it with you. If you do this and God so commands, you will be able to stand the strain, and all these people will go home satisfied. (vv. 19–23)

Jethro verifies the need for what Moses is doing. He says that the people need to be taught the law of God and understand its implications in their lives; especially their relationships with one another. But he questions Moses' method of meeting that need. He tries to enlighten Moses regarding the long-term effect of his solo approach to personnel management. He tells Moses to select godly men to help him. It is worth noting that Jethro doesn't tell Moses to just go out and "shake the bushes" to find some help. He gives him very specific qualifications for these "assistant judges," and they all have to do with character and spiritual depth.

Then he tells him how to organize this new corporation. Moses is to assume responsibility for the men under him, and he is to arrange a hierarchy of competent mediators to try the lesser cases. The difficult cases are to be brought to Moses for his personal attention. But even then, I cannot believe that the assistants would simply turn the hard cases over to him and walk away. It is very probable that they would stay and listen intently to what Moses said and how he handled the case. As a result, when a similar case came up again, they would not need to bother Moses with it.

Under this arrangement, Moses could still "measure the pulse" of the nation and maintain his sense of ultimate responsibility, yet not have the enormous strain of direct contact with every individual. It was an excellent suggestion. In a way Jethro may have been the world's first "business consultant!" He came in, assessed the situation, determined what was deficient in Moses' management style, then made suggestions—and stuck around awhile to see Moses implement the new scheme.

And in fact Moses does exactly as Jethro has advised. So Jethro returns home. Everything goes great . . . for a while. . . .

We actually see a preview of Jethro's management principle in the previous chapter (17). When the nation of Israel runs out of water, in their frustration and anger they want to kill Moses. God tells Moses to "Walk on ahead of the people. *Take with you some of the elders of Israel* and take in your hand the staff with which you struck the Nile, and go" (v. 5, emphasis added). It is very possible that God is trying to train the Israelites, the leadership, and even Moses himself, that there are others who can lead too. He may have been preparing his people to accept the idea of multiple leadership even before it was actually instituted. In this incident, Moses is still obviously the central figure, and he is the one who works the miracle. But in the eyes of the people, there is a *group* of elders associated with leadership and the meeting of needs. Moses is being "groomed" by God to delegate responsibility.

The account in Numbers 11, where we began this study, occurred about a year after the incident with Jethro. But by this time it appears that his father-in-law's sound counsel has been forgotten. Moses' complaint that, "I cannot carry all these people by myself" (v. 14) is an accurate statement. In fact, it is nearly identical to Jethro's conclusions back in Exodus 18. The burden of the multitude *was* too heavy for him. But Moses should have known what to do, from what Jethro had taught him. Instead of asking God to kill him on the spot, he should have gone to God in prayer and said, "Lord, these people are more than I can handle. There are just too many of them. Their needs outstrip my abilities. I need some help, God. Please bring me some godly men who can share this load with me." But, he doesn't. He wants to turn in his badge, sell the farm, and hang it up!

It shouldn't surprise us that God's response to Moses' request is the same answer that he gave him a year earlier: "Delegate, Moses! Delegate! And I'll even help you."

> The LORD said to Moses: "Bring me seventy of Israel's elders who are known to you as leaders and officials among the people. Have them come to the Tent of Meeting, that they may stand there with you. I will come down and speak with you there, and I will take of the Spirit that is on you and put the Spirit on them. They will help you carry the burden of the people so that you will not have to carry it alone." (Num. 11:16–17)

God is basically telling Moses that *he* will distribute the anointing of leadership to seventy others. Their leadership will be recognized by the Israelites as having its origin in God. The key difference between this account and that of Exodus 18, is that here God is telling Moses to delegate spiritual responsibilities, whereas in Exodus, Jethro's suggestions had to do with civic matters. But the principle is the same. On both occasions, Moses is trying to "do it all" alone. During the first couple of months out of Egypt, Moses was perhaps enjoying the spotlight. Carrying any load is always easiest at the start of a journey.

This "I'll do it myself" attitude appears quite frequently in Moses' life. Even when he was still living as Pharaoh's son in Egypt, he took matters into his own hands when he killed the Egyptian who was mistreating a Hebrew (Ex. 2:11–14). In the battle with the Amalekites, God granted victory to Israel as long as Moses held his arms up, from his position on a hill overlooking the battle. Eventually, others had to come and prop his arms up because he grew so fatigued. But there is no indication that Moses ever *asked* for their help. (17:8–12)

The clearest example of this independent streak occurs at the Desert of Zin in Numbers 20. Here the people of Israel discover that they have no water. They begin their normal grumbling and wishing they were back in Egypt. Moses and Aaron spread themselves prostrate before the Lord in the Tent of Meeting and plead the cause of the people. God promises Moses that he will provide water for the people. Moses has merely to "speak to that rock before their eyes and it will pour out its water" (v. 8). But when Moses leaves the Lord's presence, quite another plan moves into action:

> So Moses took the staff from the LORD's presence, just as he commanded him. He and Aaron gathered the assembly together in front of the rock and Moses said to them, "Listen, you rebels, must we bring you water out of this rock?" Then Moses raised his arm and struck the rock twice with his staff. Water gushed out, and the community and their livestock drank. (vv. 9–11)

Moses decides that he, rather than God, should get the credit for this miracle. So he not only draws attention to himself in the process, but actually changes God's specific plan and *strikes* the rock, rather than speaking to it. Maybe Moses was the inspiration for Frank Sinatra's song, "I Did It My Way"!

Going back to chapter 11, we find this do-it-yourselfer feeling totally overwhelmed and depressed. Many of us struggle with the same problem: We try to do things all by ourselves, and we tend to end up just like Moses—resentful, angry, and fatalistic. We become upset with the people we're supposedly serving. "No one cares. No one ever helps me. I've had it!" Yet too often, just like Moses, we are the ones who are to blame for the situation. And our failure can be linked to a number of key fallacies about delegating responsibility.

For the remainder of this chapter, I want to isolate these key fallacies and contrast them with the truth of what is really occurring. Then we'll construct an honest appraisal of what the real issue is—why I'm doing what I'm doing—in each case.

All of these fallacies radiate from the hub of an unwillingness on my part to delegate responsibility to those under me or around me.

FALLACY #1: "I don't have time to train someone to help."

In this case, the stereotypical answer to the question, Why don't you get someone to help you? or, Why don't you train so-and-so to do that? is, "I don't have the time to train them!" The truth of the matter is that the time it would take to train someone would be paid back very quickly. If I invest two hours to train someone to do a job that will save me only ten minutes a day, I will begin to see dividends after the first week.

This is a common source of irritation within many homes. Most parents don't feel they have the time to train their younger children to do routine chores such as laundry, dusting, or lawn work. The result is a growing irritation on the part of the parents over their children's "irresponsibility" or "ingratitude." The children, on the other hand, learn very quickly that if they let Mom and Dad fuss enough, they will do the work themselves. The opportunity to train the children never arrives, because the chores in question are usually needing to be done in the midst of the hassle and chaos that causes the conflict in the first place. Parents don't want to stop and teach their children then. And of course the "better time" to teach them never arrives. So the behavior quickly becomes a family system in which Mom and Dad yell and berate the children, yet continue to do all the work.

The real issue with this fallacy is that the competence of other people is viewed as a threat to my own indispensability. If someone else can learn to do what I'm doing, and perhaps even do it better or more efficiently, then it will only be a matter of time before I am no longer needed. This mentality, of course, is not visible, and may not even be operating on a conscious level with the person concerned. If you were to question them about it, they would tell you that the only issue at stake here is the lack of time to do the necessary training. But that's simply not true. The real issue is simply that we *want* to be indispensable. We want people to think and believe that we are the only ones who can perform certain duties.

This happened to me while running the media center at our Christian School. I slowly allowed myself to get maneuvered into a position where I was the only one who could do certain things, such as running the sound system for assemblies and maintaining the audio-visual equipment. There was virtually no one else who had my knowledge and experience. And I used to moan and complain when elementary teachers would approach me and say, "I'm putting on a musical tomorrow, and I need someone to run the sound. Would you?"

Of course I acted like I was really inconvenienced, but I actually *loved* knowing that I was indispensable to the success of the program.

I also became overwhelmed and wanted out, just like Moses.

FALLACY #2: "No one knows how to do this right except me."

This type of thinking says that I am the only person capable of accomplishing a given task the right way. Others perhaps could do the task in question, but more than likely I would have to *redo* it, to get it right. The truth is that others can do what needs to be done well enough. They may not do it perfectly; they may not meet my own standards; but they would do it well enough. I'll never forget a vacuum cleaner salesman who came to our home when we were first married. The amount of dirt he sucked out of our carpets and mattresses stunned us! After about thirty minutes of this performance, I finally asked him, "Does our home *have* to be this clean?" His vacuum cleaner was going well beyond what a vacuum cleaner really needs to do. This second fallacy operates much the same way. It demands a standard of performance that is "necessary" only to the one creating the standard. A lesser standard would allow others to do the task competently and sufficiently.

The "no one else can do it right" syndrome sometimes arises from our unwillingness to acknowledge that others can do something *differently*, and still be acceptable. We become more attached to the method than to the outcome. And when someone does an assigned task differently, we tell them they have done it incorrectly.

And we forget that ability generally improves with experience. Perhaps someone else *can't* do a certain task as well as we can. But given the opportunity and the time, they probably can. Unfortunately, many are never given the chance to improve their skills because they are either denied the opportunity from the outset, or are criticized so severely the first time they attempt it that they decide never to try again.

Although we speak of others being incapable of doing things "right," we actually mean they are incapable of doing things "my way." This mentality is prevalent in management. An executive will tell his secretary to draft a letter to a client for him. He gives her the pertinent facts and then tells her to get it done and bring to him for his signature. When the letter arrives on his desk, he promptly proceeds to edit it! He does this because the letter doesn't say it quite the way he would have written it. But the real question is, Does it say it?—not, Does it say it the way I would say it? The issue is merely one of preference. And the attitude, "No one can do it right except me!" has nothing to do with others' competence. It is a function of my own unwillingness to allow others either the opportunity to learn, or the freedom to do things differently.

FALLACY #3: "If I don't do it myself, it'll never get done!"

People with this perspective believe that those around them are lazy parasites. If the responsibilities are left up to them, they will simply remain undone. This is a common complaint of parents as well as those in the work place. But the truth is, there are always others who can do it, and who in fact *should* do it. There are always people who have the skills and ability to complete a certain task, or assume a certain responsibility. But instead, I do it, and complain, "If I didn't do such and such, it wouldn't get done!" Soon, we are overworked and angry, ready to quit, like Moses.

There are other times when something that we feel won't get done if we don't do it, *ought not to be done at all!* Think for a minute. What is the worst case scenario if the kids' beds aren't made, or the lawn goes an extra day, or even a week? The earth will still spin and human history will proceed. The excuse, "If I don't do it myself, it won't get done!" is not in itself a sufficient reason to do anything.

In the case of this fallacy, the truth is simply that the people we consider lazy probably appear that way *because we have trained them to wait.* I can still recall vividly the crew that worked for the water department where I was a chemist. Over the ten years or so that this crew had been together, the two subordinates had learned that if they waited long enough, their boss would do their job for them. Of course he swore and slammed things around as he did it, complaining, "If you want anything done right around here, you've got to do it yourself!!" But the laborers didn't mind his short tirade, because enduring it was preferable to manual labor! And of course the foreman complained to me incessantly about how lazy his two helpers were, without realizing for a moment that he had trained them that way!

FALLACY #4: "No one else has my dedication and commitment."

Remember Elijah? He told God that he was the only prophet left in all of Israel. This mistaken perspective is most commonly expressed in a sort of "martyr complex"—the attitude that everyone else is taking advantage of me. This fallacy in thinking understands commitment only in terms of visible, measurable activities. Those who are busy are committed. Those who are not busy are uncommitted.

But the truth is that I probably haven't given others a chance to develop commitment, or at least to express it. I have most likely squashed their vision and ideas with my own, or criticized their methods as unrealistic. Over time, people learn to remain silent, and eventually to be absent. But it is hardly a result of their lack of commitment. It is more a product of my inability to let go of responsibility. I have a secret passion to be in control, and entertaining others' ideas is a threat to that control. This was certainly one of the causes of Moses' discouragement. As long as he was the only person they could look to in times of spiritual crisis, he was in total control of the nation. And I suspect this was a wonderful feeling—when things were going well. But when the nation wanted to kill him, he felt overwhelmed, and the position of control and power was much less appealing and fulfilling.

I had trained my students at the Christian School to think that I was the only teacher who always had time, always understood, and was always available. Whenever they called, stayed after school, or saw me in public, I made time for them and listened intently and passionately. Over time, students came to believe that if they had a problem, I was the first person they should seek. And as my "case load" increased, so did my feelings of resentment toward my fellow teachers. I thought to myself, "Why don't *they* take time for some of these kids?!" The truth was, though I had come to believe that I was the only one who was deeply committed, I had prohibited many of my colleagues from effective ministry through my own distorted view of commitment and availability.

FALLACY #5: "The more productive I am, the better employee I am."

This fallacy believes that I can be of most use to those I serve by being as productive as I can possibly be. So I work myself to the bone, and eventually become discouraged. The truth of the matter is that if "productivity" were really the issue, it shouldn't make any difference who is being productive. If I am concerned about enhanced productivity, it shouldn't bother me that others are highly productive. Unfortunately, the real issue is that I want the attention, the approval, and the recognition that increased productivity brings.

This behavior can become nearly addictive, especially in Christian circles. There are many in the ministry who believe that the more committed they are to their ministry, the more faithful they are to God. It is a warped view of service that eventually comes to believe that "busyness" is synonymous with faithfulness. Unfortunately, it is very possible to confuse our love for God's work with our love for God. And this becomes increasingly tempting when there are visible, measurable indicators of gratitude from those we "serve." Our giving can become motivated more by the response we seek that by the service we offer.

FALLACY #6: "It's my job!"

During the years when I was burning out as a Christian high school teacher, my wife continually tried to get me to delegate or even eliminate some of my responsibilities. My standard response to her concern and suggestions was, "Jill, you just don't understand what it's like to be a teacher at a Christian school. It's my job!" Sadly, this was the same excuse I used to be so critical of in the lives of my students' parents. The father of one of my students' missed her birthday for five consecutive years. When she tearfully asked him why, his response was, "Honey, it's my job!" Now, I found myself using the same excuse.

The truth is, I had *made* those responsibilities my job. My principal didn't tell me that part of my job description involved being available for counseling during lunch, before and after school, and over the phone on weekends. In fact, when I burned out and quit teaching, and then returned, one of the first things the principal did was to tell me in no uncertain terms that I was not being hired as a counselor! What I had told my wife for three years was "my job," was *not* my job—I had simply chosen to make it my job. Rather than simply executing the duties I was hired for, I tended to migrate toward the duties that generated appreciation. Over time, they became appendages to my normal responsibilities and I couldn't discern between the expected and the extra.

These six fallacies help us understand a great deal of the discouragement that results from a failure or unwillingness to delegate responsibility. Or course not all of the six were present or obvious in the life of Moses, but the central issue is the same: The reason we don't delegate responsibility usually has to do with either an inflated or an unrealistic view of our own responsibilities or our own capacity. In my own case, I suffered from both. And the consequence was a deep discouragement and desire to quit or run away from responsibility.

It is important to realize that this failure or unwillingness to delegate is unbiblical. It is not merely unhealthy, it is contrary to the express desire of God himself. Alongside the clear examples of Moses' failure we have the positive example of the apostle Paul. The first thing Paul does on his way back from his first missionary journey is to appoint elders in the churches he has founded. Even though it is near the end of Paul's life and ministry that he provides us with the *qualifications* for elders (1 Tim. 3), he was actually appointing elders much earlier. (See Acts 14:23.)

Paul's famous statement in 2 Timothy 2:2, "The things you have heard me say in the presence of many witnesses entrust to reliable men who will also be qualified to teach others," is more than a statement of the principle of spiritual reproduction. Paul is telling Timothy to train others to share his responsibilities. "Don't try to do it alone! Delegate, Timothy!" We see this again in Ephesians 4, where Paul says that the ministry of the pastor is not to do it all. Rather, the pastor is to *equip the saints* to do it all. And it all gets done when everyone in the body is carrying their share of the load. Too often churches expect the pastor to somehow be the recipient of *all* of the spiritual gifts. He is expected to be able to preach, teach, administrate, counsel, organize, and motivate. This is very unfortunate because it creates expectations that no one can humanly meet. Yet tragically, many pastors burn out trying. They are driven to the despair that Moses felt.

Delegation of responsibility is not only necessary, it is what God wants for his people. To ignore or minimize this principle is to guarantee discouragement. Are there areas in your own life right now where you simply refuse to delegate? Are there things in your home that your children could be doing, but you won't let them because of one of those six fallacies? What about at work? Are there some duties that you simply refuse to let go that you now realize you should? "How," you ask, "can I reduce the amount of responsibility I'm carrying without actually being irresponsible?" Delegating responsibility to those to whom it actually should belong, may be the most responsible decision you can make!

Moses' cry of exasperation, "I cannot carry all these people by myself; the burden is too heavy for me," need not, indeed should not, ever come from our lips.

FOUR

Asaph:
The Foul Fruit of Comparison

"I've had it! This Christianity stuff is for the birds! The harder I try, the more I fail. The more I try to please God, the worse my life becomes. My neighbor's not a Christian; he spends all of his time on himself. He yells at his kids, never goes to church, *yet look at him!* For him things just get better and better, while my life becomes increasingly difficult and unfulfilling. I'm beginning to think that trying to be a committed Christian is a huge waste of time."

Familiar words? Frequent thoughts? Have you ever said these things or felt this way? If so, take heart—you're not alone. There is a depression that can come when we compare our life, our resources, our circumstances, and even our vocations to those of people outside the family of God. Fortunately for us, God once again has recorded for all time the struggle of a rather obscure Old Testament figure who faced this formidable foe. In fact, Asaph came as close as one can get to "throwing in the towel" in regard to his relationship with God. His story is not one of ivory tower courage. It is a testimony of both the reality of the struggle and the way to victory.

Asaph: The Man

The primary record of this little-known yet vibrant man of God is in 1 Chronicles, the historical commentary on the life of David. Here we learn a great deal about Asaph. His name appears twenty-four times in the books of Kings and Chronicles. We discover that he was among a select group of priests who were responsible for the celebration that was to accompany the bringing of the ark of the covenant back to Jerusalem (1 Chron. 15:13–19). We later discover that he was directly accountable to King David (25:6), and that he was most likely also a prophet (v. 1). Asaph was an important man of God, interacting with the king, moving in the "royal circle" in an influential manner.

Asaph was also a man of worship, a creative and deep personality who saw more than merely what his five senses told him. He saw the person and purposes of God in all of life. It is not uncommon for those who possess such intense spiritual sensitivity to fall prey to attacks from the "darker side" of the spiritual world.

We can discern the godly characteristics of Asaph from his own words. Asaph penned at least twelve of the 150 Psalms (Psalm 50 and Psalms 73–83). Probably the most familiar of these is Psalm 73. It is here, more than any other place, that Asaph's intense spiritual struggle emerges. Psalm 73 is a journal entry of one who is deeply depressed as a result of comparing himself and his life to that of the ungodly world around him. And the very fact that Asaph lived nearly three thousand years ago is a source of tremendous encouragement for those of us who share his sentiments today: Our battle is hardly new!

Asaph: His Problem

In verses 13–14 of Psalm 73, the floundering saint tells us plainly how he is feeling:

Surely in vain have I kept my heart pure;
in vain have I washed my hands in innocence.
All day long I have been plagued;
I have been punished every morning.

Asaph is convinced that all his attempts to maintain a pure relationship with God have been a waste of time. But the reason he feels his righteous life is vanity is not just because it has been difficult. Asaph is not discouraged because life has been "hard." His depression has taken root because *he* has suffered while the *wicked* seem to wend their way through life untouched by misery and pain:

They [the wicked] have no struggles;
their bodies are healthy and strong.
They are free from the burdens common to man;
they are not plagued by human ills.
Therefore pride is their necklace;
they clothe themselves with violence.
From their callous hearts comes iniquity;
the evil conceits of their minds know no limits. (vv. 4–7)

Asaph feels like a pedestrian who is continually splashed by the cars speeding by. And his feeling that the world is passing him by is not just a fleeting thought. It is the product of deep thought and speculation. Asaph has honestly tried to understand what appears to him as obvious injustice. He makes this clear in verse 16, where he says that trying to understand this incongruity has been "oppressive" to him. The Hebrew word translated oppressive carries with it the idea of pain. Asaph was feeling emotional pain from trying to understand why God would allow such an

obvious injustice, and from trying to see the worth of his righteous devotion in the face of the wicked's prosperity. In short, Asaph
was feeling that *he* was the fool rather than those who say there is
no God. (See Ps. 14:1.)

What could cause a man of such deep spiritual passion, profound spiritual experience, and significant social prestige to actually
become convinced that unrighteousness pays better dividends than
piety?

The Cause of Asaph's Pain: An Unholy Comparison

While it is abundantly clear that Asaph's depression was related
to the prosperity of the wicked and his own sense of the vanity of
righteousness, the root cause of his discouragement and depression is evident in a single statement from his own lips:

> But as for me, my feet had almost slipped;
>   I had nearly lost my foothold.
> For I envied the arrogant
>   when I saw the prosperity of the wicked. (vv. 2–3)

It was not the prosperity of the wicked that drew Asaph into
a pit of despair. In fact, it wasn't even his own personal difficulties
and trials. Asaph began to fall when he made a *comparison* between
his lot in life and that of others. He recognized this and isolated it
clearly when he said he "envied" the arrogant. Asaph's enemy was
not the arrogant or the wicked. His nemesis was his own envy.

Although it is not explicitly stated in the text, it is likely, even
probable, that the "wicked" and "arrogant" people to whom Asaph
was striking his comparison were fellow Israelites. We would like
to believe that Asaph was merely envious of blatant pagans. There
would be a sense of comfort for us if this were the case, because
such envy is obviously wrong. But Asaph's comparison was probably

with "carnal" Jews. You have to remember where Asaph spent most of his time. He was in charge of the worship associated with the ark. He spent his life around fellow Jews, helping them in their worship of sacrifices and offerings. So we can assume that Asaph's struggle was most likely not with those outside the faith.

Are not your major struggles in this area with uncommitted and carnal Christians, rather than with outright pagans? Is it not Christians who are indifferent to the demands of personal holiness and ministry, yet who seem to "have it all," who seem to have the perfect family, the perfect marriage, the perfect job . . . is it not these people who most often provoke your envy? Isn't this really where we are convinced that God is unfair? And our struggle is not so much with what they have, as it is with who we think really deserves it.

This truth has an even larger application for those of us in the vocational ministry. Asaph was "in the ministry" in the fullest sense of the word. He lived among God's people and was commissioned by the Levites and the king himself: "David left Asaph and his associates before the ark of the covenant of the LORD to minister there regularly, according to each day's requirements" (1 Chron. 16:37). Those of us in the "full-time" ministry are perhaps more prone to Asaph's ailment than "non-vocational Christians." At least one of the early apostles struggled with envy and resentment:

> Peter answered him, "We have left everything to follow you! What then will there be for us?" (Matt. 19:27)

> Peter turned and saw that the disciple whom Jesus loved was following them. . . . When Peter saw him, he asked, "Lord, what about him?" Jesus answered, "If I want him to remain alive until I return, what is that to you? You must follow me." (John 21:20–22)

It appears that the young pastor of Ephesus, Timothy, also struggled with resentment:

And the Lord's servant must not quarrel; instead, he must be kind to everyone, able to teach, not resentful. (2 Tim. 2:24)

When you are called by God to spend your entire life—all of your time, energy, and even money—seeking to meet the needs and expectations of others, you become easy prey for Satan's accusations about God's fairness and the worth of what you are doing. Why, you wonder, are you always asked to give up while others are allowed to gain?

Asaph's comparison, then, was most likely with fellow Jews who were living for themselves rather than for God . . . and were laughing all the way to the bank.

The Source of Asaph's Mistake: A Prolonged Gaze in the Wrong Direction

It is obvious from Asaph's description of those he envied that he had made a careful study of their lives. Psalm 73 should never be viewed as the passing comments of an emotional man; they are the settled conclusions of a prolonged infatuation with the life of the ungodly. Indeed Psalm 73 reads like a dissertation on "The Benefits of Being Ungodly." Asaph had studied the life of the "arrogant" and had painstakingly contrasted it with the life of the righteous. From this study he concluded that the wicked:

- lead a struggle-free life (v. 4)
- physically suffer less than the righteous (v. 5)
- are violent rather than compassionate (v. 6)
- are virtually obsessed with evil (vv. 7–8)
- are self-centered and oppressive (vv. 7–10)
- mock God, while God remains silent (vv. 9, 11)
- are admired for their evil character (v. 10)
- prosper in their wickedness (v. 12)

- are free of anxiety (v. 12)
- are much better off than he is (vv. 13–14)

Asaph's prolonged comparison of his life and that of those who lived for their own passions brought him near the edge of a dangerous precipice: "But as for me, my feet had almost slipped; I had nearly lost my foothold" (v. 2). Asaph had envied the prosperity of the ungodly, and it had initiated a downward spiral in his own relationship with God. He was depressed as a result of focusing on what they had in contrast to what he *didn't* have.

But why would this result in such a serious spiritual malaise?

The Focus Principle: A First Step Away From God?

What happened to Asaph is not limited to the spiritual life of a royal singer living nearly thirty centuries ago. Nor did it originate with him. The larger principle that helps us understand Asaph's depression actually began in the Garden with the first couple. Martin Luther captures the principle for us when he says,

> How rich a God our God is! He gives enough, but we don't notice it. He gave the whole world to Adam, but this was nothing in Adam's eyes; he was concerned about one tree and had to ask why God had forbidden him to eat of it.[8]

Satan successfully maneuvered Adam and Eve into his favorite place—focusing on what is *missing* from our lives rather than what is present. Satan's question to Eve, "Did God really say, 'You must not eat from any tree in the garden?'" was not framed to secure information. He design was to subtly shift her focus from what

---

[8]Martin Luther, quoted in *The Lutheran*, Sept. 21, 1977, 3.

was allowed to what was forbidden. In the process, Adam and Eve forgot what they *had* and could only think of what they didn't have.

This tactic is nearly foolproof. Another illustration of its power is in the life of King Ahab. He had more of everything than any of his subjects, and certainly needed nothing. Yet he became virtually obsessed with the vineyard of a man named Naboth—so much so that Naboth's unwillingness to sell it to Ahab spiralled the king into a deep depression:

> But Naboth replied, "The LORD forbid that I should give you the inheritance of my fathers."
> So Ahab went home, sullen and angry because Naboth the Jezreelite had said, "I will not give you the inheritance of my fathers." He lay on his bed sulking and refused to eat. (1 Kings 21:3–4)

The reason this tactic of the Enemy is so powerful and effective is that, in order for us to turn our focus from what we *have* to what we don't have, we must first turn our hearts away from God himself. When we focus on what we have, be it ever so small, it inevitably results in praise and thanksgiving to God. *He* becomes our focus, rather than things or people.

Thanklessness is the first step away from God. Paul spotlights this threat in the first chapter of his letter to the Romans:

> For since the creation of the world God's invisible qualities—his eternal power and divine nature—have been clearly seen, being understood from what has been made, so that men are without excuse.
> For although they knew God, they neither glorified him as God nor gave thanks to him, but their thinking became futile and their foolish hearts were darkened. Although they claimed to be wise, they became fools. (Rom. 1:20–22)

We are convinced that the larger, more noticeable sins like adultery, drunkenness, or violence are major threats to our spiritual health. But the more sobering truth is that our most significant enemies are those attitudes or behaviors that subtly shift our focus away from God. C. S. Lewis captures this truth for us in this passage from *The Screwtape Letters*, a series of fictional correspondences from an elder demon to his understudy, Wormwood:

My Dear Wormwood,

Obviously you are making excellent progress. My only fear is lest in attempting to hurry the patient [a Christian] you awaken him to a sense of his real position. For you and I, who see that position as it really is, must never forget how totally different it ought to appear to him. We know that we have introduced a change of direction in his course which is already carrying him out of his orbit around the Enemy [God]; but he must be made to imagine that all the choices which have effected this change of course are trivial and revocable. . . .

You will say that these are very small sins; and doubtless, like all young tempters, you are anxious to be able to report spectacular wickedness. But do remember, *the only thing that matters is the extent to which you separate the man from the Enemy.* It does not matter how small the sins are, provided that their cumulative effect is to edge the man away from the Light and out into the Nothing. . . . Indeed the safest road to Hell is the gradual one—the gentle slope, soft underfoot, without sudden turnings, without milestones, without signposts. (emphasis added)[9]

This idea of "focus"—where I look most intently—is what the apostle Paul calls the "set of the mind" (Rom. 8:5–8, Col. 3:1–4). He says that those who set their minds on "the flesh" (our human wants) or "the world" (this present life) will eventually die. Paul would surely agree with A. W. Tozer's definition of faith as—"the gaze of a soul upon a saving God."[10] The surest way to slowly die

---

[9]C. S. Lewis, *The Screwtape Letters* (New York: Macmillan, 1961), 53, 56.
[10]A. W. Tozer, *The Pursuit of God* (Harrisburg, Pa.: Christian Publications, 1948), 89.

spiritually, is to make anything but God our primary focus, the gaze of our soul.

Asaph had succumbed to this ancient tactic of Satan. He had allowed his mind to drift from God himself, to those around him. Even though Asaph spent his waking hours in the very tabernacle of God, he failed to "keep the LORD ever before him" (see Ps.16:8, 26:3). And as a consequence, he nearly abandoned his faith in God. But fortunately for Asaph and us, he didn't. In fact, he not only resisted the Enemy's attacks, he actually defied him and won! His winning strategy is also preserved for us in Psalm 73.

Asaph's Strategy: Two Essential Changes

Asaph's first step back toward spiritual vitality was to change his *location*. The world that threatened to smother him was left behind. We learn from verses 16–17 that he left the din of the ungodly and sought a place where he could regain his focus: "When I tried to understand all this, it was oppressive to me till I entered the sanctuary of God; then I understood their final destiny."

This is a vital lesson for us. Sometimes, in order for us to "set our minds on the things of the Spirit," we need to change our location. Going to the mall is probably not wise when we are enmeshed in financial difficulties; touring the "Parade of Homes" is the last place we should be when we're angry at God for having to rent an apartment. When God spoke most clearly to Asaph, he was away from the noise, the crowds, and the demands of others. He was alone with God. While it is true that Asaph went into an actual sanctuary (he worked nearby!), being alone with God and seeing him as our place to "hide" from the world's call is the same thing. Perhaps that is what the following Scriptures mean:

> How priceless is your unfailing love!
> Both high and low among men find refuge
>   in the shadow of your wings. (Ps. 36:7)

The LORD helps them and delivers them;
  he delivers them from the wicked and saves them,
  because they take refuge in him. (37:40)

God is our refuge and strength,
  an ever-present help in trouble. (46:1)

The first corrective step Asaph took to deliver his feet from slipping and restore his foothold of faith, was to *remove himself temporarily from the place of temptation.* Certainly he didn't abandon his responsibilities as chief singer, but he did get himself away for a time of private prayer.

The second thing that brought Asaph back to God was his change in *outlook.* As he spent time alone, thinking and praying, God began to restore to him an "eternal perspective." Asaph was able to see things in terms of their "final destiny" rather than merely their immediate status. Asaph's comments about the eventual fate of the wicked reveals that he regained a proper focus—one that sees the present in light of eternity rather than vice versa:

. . . till I entered the sanctuary of God;
  then I understood their final destiny.
Surely you place them on slippery ground;
  you cast them down to ruin.
How suddenly are they destroyed,
  completely swept away by terrors! (73:17–19)

In order to be victorious in the battle of comparison and contrast, we too must get away from the battle periodically and ask God to give us an eternal perspective—one that has a decidedly different focus, a different "gaze." God's Word tells us clearly where and at whom we should look:

Since everything will be destroyed in this way, what kind of people ought you to be? You ought to live holy and godly lives as you look forward to the day of God and speed its coming. That day will bring about the destruction of the heavens by fire, and the elements will melt in the heat. But in keeping with his promise we are looking forward to a new heaven and a new earth, the home of righteousness.

So then, dear friends, since you are looking forward to this, make every effort to be found spotless, blameless and at peace with him. (2 Peter 3:11–14)

Therefore, since we are surrounded by such a great cloud of witnesses, let us throw off everything that hinders and the sin that so easily entangles, and let us run with perseverance the race marked out for us. Let us fix our eyes on Jesus, the author and perfecter of our faith, who for the joy set before him endured the cross, scorning its shame, and sat down at the right hand of the throne of God. Consider him who endured such opposition from sinful men, so that you will not grow weary and lose heart. (Heb. 12:1–3)

We are told directly in God's Word, and illustratively through the life of Asaph, that in order to keep our own feet from slipping and our own lives from disaster, we need to maintain an eternal perspective. We must seek to keep ourselves from envying God's goodness to others, by continually drawing our own hearts back to his special goodness to us. Focusing on what we do not have is a sure beginning to turning our back on God. Asaph began to succumb to this incredible pressure until he left the scene of temptation and spent time alone with God, meditating and praying.

Asaph, however, did not stay in the sanctuary; he had to return to the "real world." So too with us. God is not merely interested in enabling us to worship him in the quiet of our refuge. He desires for us to take our revitalized eternal perspective back into the battle. For it is in the crucible of life that faith thrives best.

Four hundred years ago, Nicholas of Cusa penned this prayer:

When all my endeavour is turned toward Thee because all Thy endeavour is turned toward me; when I look unto Thee alone with all my attention, nor ever turn aside the eyes of my mind, because Thou dost enfold me with Thy constant regard; when I direct my love toward Thee alone because Thou, who are Love's self hast turned Thee toward me alone. And what, Lord, is my life, save that embrace wherein Thy delightsome sweetness doth so lovingly enfold me?[11]

---

[11]Nicholas of Cusa, quoted in Tozer, *The Pursuit of God*, 92.

FIVE

David: Dealing With Guilt

I will never forget returning home once with my four children after an especially draining day at school. I was tired, irritable, and looking for some "space."

Then I discovered that Ben, my oldest son, had failed to complete a number of basic tasks before going to school that morning. It was the final straw! I exploded into a tirade about his irresponsibility, self-centeredness, and indifference to the needs his mother and I had, trying to take care of a family of six. I was abrasive, insensitive, and unkind.

Shortly after that outburst, I went to the store. While driving, I began to relive that unfortunate encounter with my son, and began to realize that I had been seriously wrong in my actions. These feelings slowly solidified into a genuine awareness that what I had done was not only wrong—it was sin. An inner voice asked me the same questions over and over: Would Jesus have treated Ben that way? Has Jesus ever treated you that way?

Upon returning from the store, I took Ben aside and confessed to him that I was wrong, and that I had sinned against him. I asked for his forgiveness.

He said, "Dad, that's okay. You're under a lot of stress these days."

I took him by the shoulders, looked squarely at him, and responded, "Ben, Jesus would *never* have done what I did. And as far as I can tell from Scripture, he was under quite a bit of stress himself!"

That day, I encountered a deep sense of guilt, and responded by repentance and reconciliation. The guilt feelings I experienced were justified, and my response appropriate.

But are guilt feelings *always* valid? Should I respond in the same manner every time I feel guilty about something?

In the next two chapters we want to examine depression that is the product of guilt feelings. Probably no single group of people struggles with feelings of guilt more than Christians. We feel guilty for letting others down; for not measuring up; for our past; for thoughtless comments we've made. Or, we are *made* to feel guilty through the manipulative statements or behavior of other Christians. Ironically, guilt is one of the most effective and prevailing predators among a people who are supposed to be distinguished by forgiveness.

Guilt feelings paralyze us. But is the paralysis justified? In this chapter we want to examine the difference between true and false guilt, and how to deal with true guilt.

In the Court of God: Innocent or Guilty?

One of the clearest teachings of Scripture is that the genuine believer, one who has acknowledged his or her own sinfulness and has accepted the substitutionary death of Jesus Christ for sin, is totally forgiven:

> Therefore, there is now no condemnation for those who are in Christ Jesus, because through Christ Jesus the law of the Spirit of life set me free from the law of sin and death. (Rom. 8:1–2)

What, then, shall we say in response to this? If God is for us, who can be against us? He who did not spare his own Son, but gave him up for us all—how will he not also, along with him, graciously give us all things? Who will bring any charge against those whom God has chosen? It is God who justifies. (vv. 31–33)

But now he has reconciled you by Christ's physical body through death to present you holy in his sight, without blemish and free from accusation. (Col. 1:22)

The biblical doctrine of justification affirms that, because of the atoning death of Jesus Christ on my behalf, I can never be declared guilty in the court of God. There are no *degrees* of forgiveness; either I am forgiven or I am not. And if I am, it is complete, final, and irrevocable.

Not only am I not guilty, I am also declared righteous. In fact, in the transaction of faith I was given the very righteousness of Jesus himself: "God made him who had no sin to be sin for us, so that in him we might become the righteousness of God." (2 Cor. 5:21)

So final is this forgiveness that my *status* of being righteous before God can ever be jeopardized by the sins I continue to commit. I cannot lose my forgiveness. Those sins can, however, cause me to temporarily lose my fellowship with God. Sin can never take me *out* of the family of God once I am reborn into it, but it can fracture my intimacy with God—much as a misbehaving child can have a "falling out" with his father. Stated another way, genuine guilt for the Christian is more a "domestic" matter—guilt within the family of God—than a judicial matter.

Understanding this distinction will help us handle guilt as a Christian. The guilt that we struggle with as believers has nothing to do with our standing before God. It can only have to do with our relationship with him as children to their father. It is guilt within God's family. Yet even in that context, there is room for misunderstanding. There is such a thing as true and false domestic guilt.

So, as we begin to look at the Christian's struggle with guilt and guilt feelings, we need to distinguish between true guilt and false guilt. We will deal with the question of true guilt in this chapter and look at handling false guilt in the next.

For the purposes of this book, "true" guilt feelings are understood to be those that are based on a valid judgment of God. That is, they have a valid, biblical basis. They actually originate from God. "False" guilt is an invalid judgment from a source other than God.

Dealing With True Guilt

In Paul's second letter to the Corinthian church, he provides an essential principle about true guilt for the follower of Jesus Christ. Paul had confronted the Corinthians about sin in their fellowship. He was therefore dealing with actual guilt on their part. He tells them that there are two types of guilt *feelings* possible within the context of genuine guilt:

> Even if I caused you sorrow by my letter, I do not regret it. Though I did regret it—I see that my letter hurt you, but only for a little while—yet now I am happy, not because you were made sorry, but because your sorrow led you to repentance. For you became sorrowful as God intended and so were not harmed in any way by us. Godly sorrow brings repentance that leads to salvation and leaves no regret, but worldly sorrow brings death. (7:8–10)

One type of guilt feeling that Paul describes in this passage he calls "godly sorrow." The Corinthians had sinned and Paul had written to them, to confront them with the reality and seriousness of what they had done. They *were* guilty; their fellowship with God and with one another had been broken. This was true guilt. And in that context, the apostle commends them for properly responding to their guilt with godly sorrow. It is obvious from this passage that feeling guilty is not always bad—especially if in fact you are guilty. How one handles guilt feelings is really the issue, not the feelings themselves.

We can distill some of the characteristics of healthy guilt feelings from this passage. According to Paul, godly sorrow causes a change of heart and conduct. It produces a repentance that prompts a change in one's attitude and behavior. The word *repentance* in the Bible is actually a military term that means "about face," to make a 180-degree turn, to turn from sin and toward God.

Another characteristic of this godly sorrow is that it does not produce any regret. There are no, "I wish I had" or, "I wish I hadn't" residues that accompany a godly response to guilt feelings.

Godly sorrow drives us back to God, the very place our sin had led us away from.

But Paul also speaks of another type of guilt feeling, "worldly sorrow." Worldly sorrow, says Paul, causes remorse and death. This death can be emotional, spiritual, or even physical. Worldly sorrow eventually breaks our fellowship with God. It drives us away from him rather than toward him. Paul commended the Corinthians for not responding to their guilt with worldly sorrow.

A sobering truth emerges from this passage: True guilt can drive us away from God or toward him. It can yield death, or life and peace. The choice appears to be ours. Fortunately for us, the Scriptures record enlightening examples of both responses to true guilt.

Worldly Sorrow: Judas Iscariot

There are few names in the biblical record that carry the stigma and disdain of Judas Iscariot, the man who betrayed our Lord for thirty pieces of silver. He is the emblem of treason and treachery. His portrait looms large in mankind's "Hall of Shame." Although there has been a great deal of theological debate around Judas—

his place in God's plan versus the free choices he made—a number of things must be agreed upon. Judas was a real person who made real choices at real moments in history. He is not merely a paradigm of evil. Judas Iscariot was not a human puppet whose strings extended through the clouds to the hands of God. Jesus makes it clear that Judas' choices were personal and that he will be held accountable for them:

> The Son of Man will go just as it is written about him. But woe to that man who betrays the Son of Man! It would be better for him if he had not been born. (Matt. 26:24)

Judas' own behavior reveals an acute awareness that he was guilty of making some insidious choices:

> When Judas, who had betrayed him, saw that Jesus was condemned, he was seized with remorse and returned the thirty silver coins to the chief priests and the elders. "I have sinned," he said, "for I have betrayed innocent blood."
> "What is that to us?" they replied. "That's your responsibility."
> So Judas threw the money into the temple and left. Then he went away and hanged himself. (Matt. 27:3–5)

Judas' intense sense of guilt eventually caused him to turn away from God and inward upon himself. The result was an overwhelming sense of condemnation that grew into fatalism and despair. In the case of Judas, it all culminated in the ultimate act of despondency—suicide. God never designed us to be able to shoulder the full weight of our own sin and its accompanying guilt. The burden is simply too great. Judas buckled, as would any of us if we were confronted with such a stark realization of our own sin. Judas is an example of what Paul called worldly sorrow. And in his case, it indeed led to death.

How do we account for this reaction to guilt? Why didn't Judas simply go back to Jesus and at least beg for his forgiveness? What prompted him to turn his anger inward upon himself? I believe that the answers to these questions are in a couple of obscure passages of John's Gospel:

> Here a dinner was given in Jesus' honor. Martha served, while Lazarus was among those reclining at the table with him. Then Mary took about a pint of pure nard, an expensive perfume; she poured it on Jesus' feet and wiped his feet with her hair. And the house was filled with the fragrance of the perfume.
>
> But one of his disciples, Judas Iscariot, who was later to betray him, objected, "Why wasn't this perfume sold and the money given to the poor? It was worth a year's wages." He did not say this because he cared about the poor but because he was a thief; as keeper of the money bag, he used to help himself to what was put into it. (John 12: 2–6)

We learn from this passage that Judas was a thief. The force of the Greek phrase *used to help himself* implies that he habitually stole from the funds of our Lord and his disciples. He was literally robbing his friends to feather his own nest! In the scene described above, he tried to mask this greed with a pious statement about the needs of the poor, but the larger truth was that Judas had already become callous to human need. He didn't care one iota about the poor. But, there was an even more serious consequence of his thievery.

One of the unfortunate side-effects of continually neglecting the subtle prompting of our conscience, as Judas had undoubtedly done, is the gradual darkening and distortion of our understanding of the character of God. As we continue to ignore his attempts to call us back to that which we know is right, a growing sense of distance develops between us and God. For the person who refuses to heed his conscience, God eventually becomes a stranger rather than a friend. It becomes increasingly difficult, and eventually impossible to go to God in time of need . . . because of all the obstacles that clutter the path.

Judas would have had to confess an entire *series* of sins to our Lord before he could begin to confess his sin of betrayal. And the enormity of that task discouraged him from even trying. The outcome, of course, was fatal.

Listen to how the apostle Paul describes the disastrous results of not heeding our conscience:

> Timothy, my son, I give you this instruction in keeping with the prophecies once made about you, so that by following them you may fight the good fight, holding on to faith and a good conscience. Some have rejected these and so have shipwrecked their faith. (1 Tim. 1:18–19)

Neglecting our conscience can "shipwreck" our faith and destroy our relationship with God. A shipwreck is not simply a leak in a rubber raft! It means the loss of the ship, the loss of life, the loss of everything. Certainly Judas demonstrates this principle in technicolor.

Judas responded to his feelings of true guilt with "worldly sorrow" and it ended in death. But the Bible also shows us a second way to handle guilt feelings—one that has less disastrous, even wonderful results.

Godly Sorrow: King David

2 Samuel 11 contains one of the most familiar and yet tragic stories in all of Scripture. King David, a "man after God's own heart," made a couple of fatal choices that launched him into a spiral of sin that tarnished an entire nation. The noticeable portion of it began one night as he walked on the roof of his palace and noticed a young woman bathing. Rather than turning his gaze away, he let it grow into a raging lust. He summoned this woman to

his palace, knowing full well that she was the wife of one of his most faithful men. Then, he committed adultery with her.

Lust knows no bounds, and what began as a private sin evolved into a debacle. David began a series of lies and political intrigue that eventually culminated in the death of Bathsheba's husband, an unwanted pregnancy, and the death of the unwanted child. David's sin was great, but as is always the case with moral sin, its consequences were greater.

In the next chapter of 2 Samuel, the prophet Nathan is directed by God to confront David with his sin. David's response to Nathan's rebuke is one of "godly sorrow," for he is broken and shattered by his disobedience. It would be safe to say that David *felt* as much guilt as Judas. Yet his response is totally different. It is obvious by David's response to Nathan that he had already been engaged in an intense battle with his guilt. In fact Psalm 51, which David wrote after Nathan had confronted him, contains a great deal of insight about David's "godly sorrow." From it we learn that David's sin had haunted him daily (v. 3); that he had come to realize that his very *heart* was sinful (vv. 5–6, 10); and that he had lost all joy in his relationship with God (v. 12). David was consumed with guilt and it had poisoned his joy and desiccated his walk with the Lord.

But instead of turning away from God and in upon himself, like Judas would do nearly ten centuries later, David turned his heart *toward* God. He acknowledged his sin, and asked God to change his sinful heart:

> Cleanse me with hyssop, and I will be clean;
>   wash me, and I will be whiter than snow.
> Let me hear joy and gladness;
>   let the bones you have crushed rejoice.
> Hide your face from my sins and blot out all my iniquity.
> Create in me a pure heart, O God,
>   and renew a steadfast spirit within me. (vv. 7–10)

This is what godly sorrow looks like. It ultimately ends in forgiveness, hope, and joy. David stood full stature in the mirror of God's conviction and acknowledged the reality of his sinful heart and what it had led to. Too often, when God begins to "put his finger on us" for some sin in our lives, we immediately look for someone else to blame. Adam blamed Eve; Eve blamed the serpent (Gen. 3); Aaron blamed the Israelites for the golden calf (Ex. 32:22–24); and Saul blamed his soldiers for pressuring him to disobey God (1 Sam. 13:11–12). And we've done the same thing many times. But in this instance, David didn't. He faced his guilt and took it *back to God* rather than away from him. That is the essential difference between godly sorrow and worldly sorrow: One takes its guilt to God, the other away from him.

Knowing the difference between these two responses to guilt, however, does not explain why Judas and David responded as they did. As already suggested, I believe that the key to understanding the difference in their responses has to do with how many obstacles they had to remove to get back to God. In the case of Judas, the path to God was cluttered with unconfessed sin. For him to repent of his sin of betrayal, he would have first had to tell the Lord about his sins of disloyalty, theft, deceit, hypocrisy . . . the list was surely quite lengthy, and the task of dealing with it must have seemed too large and difficult to Judas. The path away from God was much easier.

David, on the other hand, found the path back to God to be relatively uncluttered. Even though his sins were heinous, they were not numerous. He could "see" the way back to the Lord; Judas couldn't have seen his way even if he had wanted to. We learn from 1 Kings 15:5 that "David had done what was right in the eyes of the LORD and had not failed to keep any of the LORD's commands all the days of his life—except in the case of Uriah the Hittite" (Bathsheba's husband). It is obvious that David must have been in the habit of keeping "short accounts" with God; of confessing known sin as soon as he became aware of it rather than letting it accumulate as Judas had done. David had a desire to stay in fellowship with God; he didn't want any distance to develop.

David did not neglect his conscience, and therefore did not make shipwreck of his faith. Listening to our conscience, that spiritual link between us and the Lord, is a crucial factor in responding to true guilt with godly sorrow. If we separate ourselves from fellowship with God over a long period of time, we will respond to genuine guilt as Judas did, by turning away from the Lord and inward upon ourselves. The result will be depression, loneliness, and perhaps even despair and death.

But if we are faithful to keep short accounts with God, by listening to our conscience, we can take our guilt feelings to him instead of away from him. The result, according to David himself, is peace and joy:

> Blessed is the man whose transgressions are forgiven,
>   whose sins are covered.
> Blessed is the man whose sin the Lord does not
>   count against him and in whose spirit is no deceit.

SIX

David:
Dealing With False Guilt

In the last chapter, we saw that there is such a thing as "true domestic guilt" in regard to our relationship with the Lord. This type of guilt produces a genuine sense of conviction from God, because it has a valid basis. True guilt can produce godly sorrow, which leads to repentance and restored fellowship with God, or worldly sorrow, which leads to separation from God and even death.

There is another type of guilt that causes sorrow for the Christian, perhaps even more so than true domestic guilt. This *false* guilt produces a gnawing sense of condemnation rather than conviction. The condemnation involves two primary ingredients: an acute sense of personal failure, and an awareness of the need for justice to be served, for punishment to be executed.

False guilt is false for two reasons. First and foremost, it is false because of its source. God and God alone has the authority to pronounce us guilty; and as we have noted and shall shortly examine in more detail, false guilt always comes from an invalid source.

Second, the feelings of condemnation caused by false guilt always have to do with punishment, and there is no punishment left for the true disciple of Jesus Christ. He took *all* of our punishment for us on the Cross. There is no "unfinished business" between us and God. Our standing with God is as secure as God himself. Our *fellowship* with God can be broken, but never the fact of our adoption as his sons and daughters.

According to Hebrews 12:5–13, God's present involvement in our sin never has to do with punishment. He "disciplines" us for our sin, but the goal of this discipline is not punishment. It is not the exacting of payment for a wrong committed. Rather, the goal of God's *discipline* is our *discipleship*. The goal is that we should conform more closely to the image of Jesus Christ. Any guilt that makes me feel that I deserve to be punished, that I'm a failure, or that "I've got this coming" is a false guilt by virtue of the fact that it has to do with punishment. Punishment is no longer an issue for true believers.

False guilt feelings—feelings of accusation or condemnation—are not only invalid, they constitute an assault on the sufficiency of the atoning work of Jesus Christ. Such feelings are much more than merely a personal problem. They involve an attack on the very heart of Christianity.

The Sources of False Guilt

False guilt comes from one of only three significant sources. Oddly, the first and most frequent and forceful origin of false guilt is ourselves. Many Christians are their own worst enemy when it comes to the battle with false guilt. Even in the first century, Christians were battling with the devastating impact of self-condemnation:

> This then is how we know that we belong to the truth, and how we set our hearts at rest in his presence whenever our hearts condemn us. For God is greater than our hearts, and he knows everything. (1 John 3:19–20)

> For it is not the one who commends himself who is approved, but the one whom the Lord commends. (2 Cor. 10:18)

While it is true that the Bible exhorts us to examine ourselves and to check our motives and values, even to probe the genuineness of our faith,[12] such examination is always for the purpose of growth, never for condemnation and judgment. Too often, when we conduct self-evaluations, they produce harm rather than help.

Sadly, our own opinion of ourselves is often the most ravaging source of accusation in our lives. This is understandable because, other than God, we are the only ones who are aware of the *extent* of our own depravity and sin. When we make ourselves the final judge of ourselves, accusation and condemnation inevitably result. The only other option is an inflated sense of righteousness, which of course is pride. Either way, we end up feeling guilty for who we are.

This self-condemnation is bad enough, but it is compounded by a second source of condemnation—others, particularly other *Christians*. The statements, implications, and insinuations of other Christians can lead to false guilt. The role of judge that we use on ourselves is easily turned outward on others. Christians tend to be the most judgmental and critical people on earth. Even the apostle Paul, writing in the middle of the first century, faced this phenomenon with the people he was ministering to in Rome:

> You, then, why do you judge your brother? Or why do you look down on your brother? For we will all stand before God's judgment seat. It is written: "'As surely as I live,' says the Lord, 'every knee will bow before me; every tongue will confess to God.'" So then, each of us will give an account of himself to God.
>
> Therefore let us stop passing judgment on one another. Instead, make up your mind not to put any stumbling block or obstacle in your brother's way. (Rom. 14:10–13)

Sometimes we can create guilt feelings in others through our expectations, spoken or unspoken. Too often we have higher

---

[12]Lam. 3:40, 1 Cor. 11:28, 2 Cor. 13:5, Gal. 6:4.

standards than God himself regarding what we want people to be and do. The apostle Peter spoke out against unrealistic expectations in the early church. When the predominantly Jewish church was beginning to extend the gospel to Gentiles, the Jewish Christians wanted to immediately impose a list of expected behaviors on the new Gentile converts—the very list that had produced their own intense guilt feelings for failing to keep it! Peter pointed out the fallacy of such reasoning when he said to the Jewish Christians,

> "He made no distinction between us and them, for he purified their hearts by faith. Now then, why do you try to test God by putting on the necks of the disciples a yoke that neither we nor our fathers have been able to bear? No! We believe it is through the grace of our Lord Jesus that we are saved, just as they are." (Acts 15:9–11)

The tragedy of such unrealistic expectations for Christian behavior is seen most acutely in relationships between Christian parents and their children. Too often, parents fail to account for the very real doctrine of depravity in their children on the one hand, and their own failure to practice what they preach on the other. Many children, burdened down by the guilt these unbiblical expectations produce, mistakenly decide to abandon their faith altogether, thinking that it is the source of their frustration.

A third debilitating source of false guilt, one whose power is primarily due to the fact that it is unseen, is Satan and his angels. We know from the story of Job that Satan is actually *looking* for opportunities to dismantle individual believers. Peter amplifies this truth when he says, "Be self-controlled and alert. Your enemy the devil prowls around like a roaring lion looking for someone to devour." (1 Peter 5:8)

Because of its paralyzing effects, false guilt is one of Satan's primary weapons. Of course it is impossible that Satan is *personally* dealing with each of us. He is not all-present like God, and cannot be in more than one location at a time. Any spiritual harassment we experience is most likely due to the attacks of his emissaries—the demonic hosts. Nor can Satan or his demons accomplish anything in our lives that God has not given them permission to do—unless we are outside of God's protective "umbrella" due to our own willful sin.

The method Satan and his angels use to create false guilt is captured for us in the names he is given in Scripture:

Then I heard a loud voice in heaven say:

"Now have come the salvation and the power
 and the kingdom of our God,
 and the authority of his Christ.
For the accuser of our brothers,
 who accuses them before our God day and night,
 has been hurled down." (Rev. 12:10)

Satan is the accuser. And more often than not, his accusations are true! Satan revels in reminding us of the truth about ourselves *while deliberately neglecting to remind us of the truth about God.* One of the quickest ways to become enveloped in false guilt is to meditate on your own character apart from your righteous standing with God in Christ. Satan is a master at that tactic.

So, the three primary sources of accusation that lead to feelings of condemnation are ourselves, others, and Satan. How do we deal with such intense feelings? How do we confront these three powerful forces of defeat in our lives? The surest way to confront them is to understand whether or not there is any validity to their threats.

Who Can Condemn Me?

A recent television comedy special featured a well-known comedian dressed up in a mock police uniform, walking the sidewalks of America's cities as a member of the "fashion police." He stopped random individuals and gave them "tickets" for violating a supposed fashion code. Most of those drawn into this comical fiasco were incredulous at first, but eventually laughed because of the absurdity of the idea. They simply ruled out the possibility of guilt because of the nature of the source. The same is true in the arena of false guilt. If we can convince ourselves that the *source* of our guilt feelings is invalid, then we can attempt to deal with what is left—the feelings themselves.

We said that one of the most persistent sources of condemnation is ourselves. Can we legitimately condemn ourselves? Are our own self-accusations valid? God's Word says no.

First of all, we need to view our self-accusations in the light of our Lord's continual testimony before God in our defense:

> My dear children, I write this to you so that you will not sin. But if anybody does sin, we have one who speaks to the Father in our defense—Jesus Christ, the Righteous One. (1 John 2:1)

When I attempt to malign my own character, Jesus Christ speaks to the Father *on my behalf*. My own accusations are "overruled" in the court of heaven!

But there is an even more liberating truth in Scripture regarding the merit of my self-condemnation:

> I have been crucified with Christ and I no longer live, but Christ lives in me. The life I live in the body, I live by faith in the Son of God, who loved me and gave himself for me. (Gal. 2:20)

Paul tells us that both the person passing judgment and the one on whom judgment is passed (the "old me" in both cases), are

dead! When Jesus Christ hung on the Cross, we hung there with
him. That means that, in legal terms, *there is no accused!* For the
Christian to condemn himself is the equivalent of putting a corpse
on trial. The one who is deemed guilty has already been "crucified
with Christ."

In short, my own self-condemnation is not just invalid—it is
impossible.

How about the false feelings of guilt that come from the comments and implications of others, particularly of other Christians?
Do they have the right to pronounce judgment on me? Can I legitimately pass judgment on other believers? The apostle Paul makes
a sweeping statement in his letter to the Romans that provides a
swift and severe warning to all who would judge others within the
faith:

> You, therefore, have no excuse, you who pass judgment on someone
> else, for at whatever point you judge the other, you are condemning
> yourself, because you who pass judgment do the same things.
> (Rom. 2:1)

James takes the explanation a step further. He says that when
we pronounce final judgment on others, particularly other believers, we are assuming the role of God:

> Brothers, do not slander one another. Anyone who speaks against
> his brother or judges him speaks against the law and judges it.
> When you judge the law, you are not keeping it, but sitting in judg-
> ment on it. There is only one Lawgiver and Judge, the one who is
> able to save and destroy. But you—who are you to judge your
> neighbor? (James 4:11–12)

In essence, Paul and James are saying that judging others is
invalid because in order to do so, I have to assume innocence on
my part. And Paul makes it clear that if someone else is truly guilty
for what they've done, I share their condemnation, for I do the

same things. And if *everyone* is guilty (which he goes on to establish in Romans 3), then no one can be innocent. So, the grounds for passing judgment are done away with. In order for true judgment to occur, there must be purity in the one supposing to pass judgment. And in the case of human beings, Paul settles it once and for all when he says, "What shall we conclude then? Are we any better? Not at all! We have already made the charge that Jews and Gentiles alike are all under sin" (Romans 3:9). The condemnation that is forced upon us, and that which we attempt to foist upon others, has no basis in truth. It, too, is invalid.

Of course the fact that we have neither the right nor the authority to pronounce a final judgment on anyone, including ourselves, should not be confused with our biblical responsibility to help other believers deal with sin in their lives. Scripture is clear that we are often blind to various sins in our own lives, and are actually dependent upon others to help us see them (Heb. 3:13). But God is also very clear in providing us with instructions regarding the proper spirit or attitude we should exhibit when undertaking such a difficult task:

> Brothers, if someone is caught in a sin, you who are spiritual should restore him gently. But watch yourself, or you also may be tempted. Carry each other's burdens, and in this way you will fulfill the law of Christ. (Gal. 6:1–2)

We have the responsibility to restore, but never the right to condemn.

The third potent source of guilt feelings is Satan and his hosts. We have vivid proof of the intensity and success with which he and his minions operate from the life of Job and of our Lord. It is Satan's goal to show no mercy and take no survivors. But are his accusations valid?

The extent and nature of Satan's authority is one of the more misunderstood facets of Christian theology. It appears that many

Christians distill their understanding of Satan from Gary Larson's *Far Side* cartoons rather than from the Bible. One common misconception, fueled by Larson and by cartoonists in general, is that Satan is "in charge" of hell. We have come to believe that he is its "boss," instead of recognizing that hell was created as a place of torment for Satan and the fallen angels (Matt. 25:41). Those who spend eternity in hell will not do so under Satan's scrutiny and control. They will merely be co-residents with him.

Scripture consoles us with an abundance of clear statements about the extent of our Enemy's authority and power:

> Since the children have flesh and blood, he [Christ] too shared in their humanity so that by his death he might destroy him who holds the power of death—that is, the devil—and free those who all their lives were held in slavery by their fear of death. (Heb. 2:14–15)

> And having disarmed the powers and authorities, he made a public spectacle of them, triumphing over them by the cross. (Col. 2:15)

> You, dear children, are from God and have overcome them [spirits of antichrist], because the one who is in you is greater than the one who is in the world. (1 John 4:4)

Satan's clearest advantage over us is our own misconceptions about his authority and power. The ultimate power he held was the power of death, and Jesus Christ conquered that power through his resurrection. Satan has no authority to punish, and therefore no authority to condemn. In the words of Martin Luther, he is merely "God's errand boy." Any guilt that is derived from his harassing accusations is false guilt. While it can be effective by virtue of its intensity, accuracy, and sheer persistence, it is false nonetheless because its source is invalid.

A fourth source of false guilt, one that is actually a weapon for the previous three, is the Law of God—that body of rules and regulations by which people's behavior is measured and judged. We are

constantly measuring ourselves and others by God's standards—
with the misdirected purpose of verifying failure. The Law of God,
which Paul says was intended to drive us to Christ (Gal. 3:24),
quickly becomes a whip in our own hands and that of our Enemy,
driving us farther *from* him.

But even the Law of God cannot condemn us, because in Christ
we meet all its requirements:

> For what the law was powerless to do in that it was weakened by the
> sinful nature, God did by sending his own Son in the likeness of sin-
> ful man to be a sin offering. And so he condemned sin in sinful man,
> *in order that the righteous requirements of the law might be fully met in
> us,* who do not live according to the sinful nature but according to
> the Spirit. (Rom. 8:3–4, emphasis added)

There are absolutely no grounds for me to be condemned any
longer. The requirements of the law have been met, once and for all,
in the substitutionary death of Jesus Christ.

There is only one source of legitimate judgment upon us. And
that is God himself. We know from Scripture that God is holy and
pure, refusing to tolerate evil in his presence (1 Sam. 6:20) and
demanding holiness in us (Heb. 12:14). James tells us soberly,
"There is only one Lawgiver and Judge, the one who is able to save
and destroy" (James 4:12). Certainly, if we were to expect and fear
judgment from anyone, it would be from God. Yet the resounding
message of the Bible is that the God who stands as Judge is also
the God who is our Advocate (1 John 2:1–2). The very One who
could justly exact the death penalty from us has already paid that
penalty—himself!

> What, then, shall we say in response to this? If God is for us, who
> can be against us? He who did not spare his own Son, but gave him
> up for us all—how will he not also, along with him, graciously give
> us all things? Who will bring any charge against those whom God
> has chosen? It is God who justifies. Who is he that condemns?
> Christ Jesus, who died—more than that, who was raised to life—is

at the right hand of God and is also interceding for us. (Rom. 8:31–34)

Elsewhere, Paul elaborates even further on the impossibility of God condemning us:

Once you were alienated from God and were enemies in your minds because of your evil behavior. But now he has reconciled you by Christ's physical body through death to present you holy in his sight, without blemish and free from accusation—if you continue in your faith, established and firm, not moved from the hope held out in the gospel. This is the gospel that you heard and that has been proclaimed to every creature under heaven, and of which I, Paul, have become a servant. (Col. 1:21–23)

It is obvious that, for genuine Christians, any condemnation we *feel* from ourselves, others, Satan, and even the Law of God is invalid and therefore nothing more than our emotional response to accusation. The only valid source of condemnation is God, and he is the one who has declared us free from accusation.

Condemnation and Conviction: Is There a Difference?

There is no one to condemn us, and yet we often *feel* condemned. Feelings of condemnation attack the notion of our adoption by God as his children. Such feelings are invalid because, as we have seen, our status as God's sons and daughters is fixed, forever. But what about those times when our *fellowship* with our heavenly Father is broken?

The mechanism God uses to alert us to the fact that our *fellowship* with him is genuinely fractured is what is known as *conviction*. Conviction produces true guilt feelings, while condemnation yields false guilt feelings. Here are some of the key distinctions between the condemnation and conviction:

CONDEMNATION	CONVICTION
1. Comes from sources other than God.	1. Comes from God, either directly through the Holy Spirit in our own hearts, or through the Spirit's use of God's Word. God can also use secondary vehicles such as books, music, or other believers.
2. Attacks who I *am* (or appear to be).	2. Reminds me of what I've *done* (my behavior). (Isa. 59:1–2)
3. Is often relentless and vague.	3. Is reasonable and specific. (Isa. 1:18, 2 Sam. 12:1–9)
4. Offers no possible relief.	4. Offers immediate freedom upon confession. (1 John 1:9)

One of the ways we contribute most to our battle with false guilt is our ignorance of the nature of genuine conviction. The Bible teaches clearly that the Holy Spirit is the only vehicle of genuine conviction from God. It is not our job to "dig up dirt" from our pasts, nor to painfully search for sin in the present. One of the clearest truths of God's Word is that if we set our hearts on being like Christ, he will alert us to sin:

> Brothers, I do not consider myself yet to have taken hold of it. But one thing I do: Forgetting what is behind and straining toward what is ahead, I press on toward the goal to win the prize for which God has called me heavenward in Christ Jesus.

> All of us who are mature should take such a view of things
> [pressing on]. *And if on some point you think differently, that too God*
> *will make clear to you.* Only let us live up to what we have already
> attained.(Phil. 3:13–16, emphasis added; see also John 14:25–26,
> 16:13–14)

God will "make clear" to us, anything we need to be convicted of.

Our age is characterized by a multitude of methods and motives
for searching out our collective and individual pasts. God tells us to
forget the past, unless he brings it to our attention. Ironically, one
of the primary ministries of the Holy Spirit—the conviction of sin
in the life of the believer—has too often been replaced by well-
meaning people.

Certainly one of the causes of our confusion over true conviction is our misunderstanding of whose responsibility it is to reveal
sin. But another source of this confusion is our ignorance regarding
what true, Spirit-filled conviction looks like. What can we expect
when God is convicting us of sin? Genuine conviction from God is
actually nothing more or less than godly wisdom—the ability to
see life as God sees it. And James 3:17 gives us a detailed description of godly wisdom:

> The wisdom from above is first pure, then peaceable, gentle, open to
> reason, full of mercy and good fruits, without uncertainty or insin-
> cerity. (RSV)

Contrast these characteristics with those that accompany feelings of false guilt. False guilt is disturbing rather than peaceable;
harsh rather than gentle; accusatory rather than open to reason;
condemning rather than full of mercy; and vague rather than certain
and specific. When God's Spirit puts the light of conviction on a
dark spot in our behavior or character, he does so with such grace
and blessing that our response is one of, "Yes, Lord, I agree."

False guilt, the gnawing corrosion of our spirits and hopes by
ourselves, others, or the agents of darkness, is a key weapon in the

arsenal of the Enemy of our souls. It paralyzes us and makes us impotent for God. The surest defense against false guilt is to recognize the invalidity of its sources, and to recognize true conviction when God brings it into our lives. Our ability to do both is the natural fruit of a vital relationship with God. In fact, the ability to distinguish good from evil, an essential prerequisite to knowing when we *have* sinned, is the result of training our consciences to respond to God:

> We have much to say about this, but it is hard to explain because you are slow to learn. In fact, though by this time you ought to be teachers, you need someone to teach you the elementary truths of God's word all over again. You need milk, not solid food! Anyone who lives on milk, being still an infant, is not acquainted with the teaching about righteousness. But solid food is for the mature, who by constant use have trained themselves to distinguish good from evil. (Heb. 5:11–14)

The writer of Hebrews makes it abundantly clear that being able to distinguish good from evil (or truth from falsehood, for that matter) comes from repeated opportunities to *use* the "solid food" of God's Word as a standard. And obviously that is impossible without a steady diet of Scripture. How are your own "eating habits" lately?

SEVEN

Israel:
Looking to the Past

> Man hath a weary pilgrimage
>   As through the world he wends,
> On every stage, from youth to age,
>   Still discontent attends;
> With heaviness he casts his eye
>   Upon the road before,
> And still remembers with a sigh
>   The days that are no more.
>
> —Robert Southey, *Remembrance*[13]

In this chapter, rather than studying one particular biblical character who was depressed, we want to examine the nation of Israel as a whole. We'll see how God's chosen nation exemplifies a common cause of discouragement for Christians.

Israel had a perennial habit that was a source of repeated disheartenment to them, and of consternation to God. They

---

[13]Robert Southey, quoted in Burton Stevenson, ed., *The Home Book of Quotations*, (New York: Greenwich House, 1984), 1460.

succumbed to the pitfall described in Robert Southey's poem. And it had indeed produced a sense of "heaviness" as they cast their collective "eye upon the road before." As a nation, Israel had constantly attempted to live today and plan for the future . . . with their focus on the past. Winston Churchill's maxim, "If we open a quarrel between the past and the present, we shall discover that we have lost the future," could easily have been Israel's motto.

As is always the case with those who focus on the past, Israel became disillusioned and despondent—even fatalistic. Why? What was their real problem, and its causes?

The "Myth of Nostalgia"

One of the most common pitfalls that we, like Old Testament Israel, stumble into in the face of adversity is what might be called the "myth of nostalgia." It is an acute form of selective memory. We choose what to remember and what to forget, in regards to our understanding of God. And by comparison, the past always seems to have been a happier, more preferable time—even though it usually was not. This causes depression in our lives because it paralyzes us in the present, thereby destroying any vision of the future—and with that loss of vision goes any possibility of genuine hope. Israel as a nation provides us with a number of cameos of this debilitating process in operation. Probably the best example emerges shortly after their miraculous Exodus from bondage in Egypt.

After witnessing God's incredible power in the ten plagues, and his faithfulness at the Red Sea, the people of God are confronted with their first real test of faith:

> Then Moses led Israel from the Red Sea and they went into the Desert of Shur. For three days they traveled in the desert without finding water. When they came to Marah, they could not drink its water because it was bitter. (That is why the place is called Marah.)

So the people grumbled against Moses, saying, "What are we to drink?"

Then Moses cried out to the LORD, and the LORD showed him a piece of wood. He threw it into the water, and the water became sweet. (Ex. 15:22–25)

You can imagine what the Israelites are discussing among themselves, meandering through the wilderness. The majesty of God's might at the Red Sea has been slowly but surely replaced by the reality of their crying children, their weary animals, and the unavoidable realization that their own tongues are sticking to the roofs of their mouths. They begin to question the value of "miracles" that only lead to death in the desert.

Having partaken of the waters at Marah, the multitude travels into the Wilderness of Sin, and after about a week they realize that they are now without food:

The whole Israelite community set out from Elim and came to the Desert of Sin, which is between Elim and Sinai, on the fifteenth day of the second month after they had come out of Egypt. In the desert the whole community grumbled against Moses and Aaron. (16:1–2)

Faced with the genuine possibility of starvation, the second major threat to their lives within just a few weeks, the Jews begin to entertain feelings of nostalgia. The myth of nostalgia causes us to view our past, even with all its pain and hardship, as pleasant in comparison to the difficulties of the present. The problem with this myth is that what we choose to recall about the past is always quite different from what really happened and how we really felt when it was happening.

And the bias is always in favor of the past. Let's take a look at the people of Israel as they succumb to the myth of nostalgia.

Egypt: The Rameses Hilton, or Hardship?

In the face of starvation, Moses' murmuring multitude recounts for him their recollection of the time spent in Egypt just a few months earlier. Their description reads like a travel brochure:

> The Israelites said to them, "If only we had died by the LORD's hand in Egypt! There we sat around pots of meat and ate all the food we wanted, but you have brought us out into this desert to starve this entire assembly to death." (v. 3)

We get the distinct impression that the Jews had been dragged from a life of leisure, a perpetual fondue feast of kosher food, good wine, and pleasant conversation. Somewhere between the Sinai peninsula and the Desert of Sin, they had begun to suffer from partial amnesia. We have an accurate description of their life in Egypt preserved for us in the first chapter of the same book that contains their carefully edited version:

> So they put slave masters over them to oppress them with forced labor, and they built Pithom and Rameses as store cities for Pharaoh. But the more they were oppressed, the more they multiplied and spread; so the Egyptians came to dread the Israelites and worked them ruthlessly. They made their lives bitter with hard labor in brick and mortar and with all kinds of work in the fields; in all their hard labor the Egyptians used them ruthlessly. (Ex. 1:11–14)

Facing the possibility of *no* food, the Jews can only remember that they *had* food in Egypt. Feeling abandoned and neglected, the abusive attention they received while Pharaoh's slaves seems like a lost blessing. They have blocked out the oppressive and bitter circumstances in which they had eaten.

Another excellent illustration of the myth of nostalgia occurs nearly two years later:

> The rabble with them began to crave other food, and again the Israelites started wailing and said, "If only we had meat to eat! We

remember the fish we ate in Egypt at no cost—also the cucumbers, melons, leeks, onions and garlic. But now we have lost our appetite; we never see anything but this manna!" (Num. 11:4–6)

In response to their earlier grumbling, God had granted them manna, a perfect source of nutrition which required no effort or preparation. Now, two years later, they are no longer facing starvation, but monotony! They are "fed up" with the manna. They are craving some variety in their diet. And predictably, their thoughts once again drift back to the "good old days" when they had choices on their menu. And their recollection of the "salad bar" at the Rameses Hilton is no less tainted with nostalgia than their memory two years earlier. Perhaps the time span has even clouded their minds further. For the account of Egypt given us in Exodus doesn't sound quite the same:

Then Pharaoh gave this order to all his people: "Every boy that is born you must throw into the Nile, but let every girl live." (Ex. 1:22)

During that long period, the king of Egypt died. The Israelites groaned in their slavery and cried out, and their cry for help because of their slavery went up to God. (2:23)

In their backward glance over their shoulders, the Israelites conveniently excluded the bigger picture from view. Egypt may have had food and a diet with variety, but it was also an oppressive tomb from which had they pleaded with God for deliverance. The pain of their corporate past in Egypt was masked by the fact that it had provided something for them that was lacking from their present experience. The Egypt they longed for had never really existed, beyond their clouded recollections. Nonetheless, it successfully poisoned their view of the present.

I recall a period in our lives when Jill and I were consumed with loneliness in the church we were attending. In an attempt to deal with the pain, we would frequently "drift back" to our days before seminary, when we had lived in a small midwestern town. Life was bliss—or so our recollection sought to convince us. Actually, that had been a time of great frustration as well. Our loneliness then was not from the absence of close friends, but from our inability to find couples our age who shared our spiritual values and vision. However, with a few years gone by, the loneliness of that era was camouflaged, and our only recollection was of the variety of people who had populated our personal world at the time. Facing the harsh reality of no friends, the past took on a distorted and enviable form.

The myth of nostalgia can stalk us when something we had is taken away from us, and also when something we have is simply diminished in some way. When the Jewish temple was destroyed by the Babylonians in the sixth century before Christ, most of the Jews were deported to captivity in Babylon. Eventually some were allowed to return to their homeland. The story is preserved for us in the books of Ezra and Nehemiah. After returning, the enormous task of rebuilding the temple was begun. In 515 B.C. the task was completed. The responses of the younger and older Jews is very revealing in regard to the nostalgia principle:

> When the builders laid the foundation of the temple of the LORD, the priests in their vestments and with trumpets, and the Levites (the sons of Asaph) with cymbals, took their places to praise the LORD, as prescribed by David king of Israel. With praise and thanksgiving they sang to the LORD: "He is good; his love to Israel endures forever." And all the people gave a great shout of praise to the LORD, because the foundation of the house of the LORD was laid. But many of the older priests and Levites and family heads, who had seen the former temple, wept aloud when they saw the foundation of this temple being laid, while many others shouted for joy. (Ezra 3:10–12)

Further insight is gained from the prophet Haggai, who ministered during this same time period:

On the twenty-first day of the seventh month, the word of the LORD came through the prophet Haggai: "Speak to Zerubbabel son of Shealtiel, governor of Judah, to Joshua son of Jehozadak, the high priest, and to the remnant of the people. Ask them, 'Who of you is left who saw this house in its former glory? How does it look to you now? Does it not seem to you like nothing?'" (Hag. 2:1–3)

Once again, as in the wilderness, Israel's focus was on the past rather than where it belonged.

But where *did* their focus belong? What was the root cause of their succumbing once again to nostalgia? They had, in fact, become victims of a danger God had warned them about repeatedly. Their failure must be our warning. For we can fall prey to the same temptation.

The Real Problem: Forgetting God

The Lord knew from the very beginning that Israel would have a problem with "selective recall"—remembering only what it wanted to rather than what it should. In fact, at least eighteen times from the time they left Egypt until they entered the land of Canaan, God commanded them to "remember" either their bondage, his miraculous deliverance, or his Law.[14] It was almost as though God was hinting to them that their biggest enemy ahead would not be thirst, famine, or the Canaanites—it would be their tendency to forget him and his mighty deeds.

And he was right, of course. Near the end of Israel's "glory years," just prior to the destruction of Jerusalem and the temple, and the nation's captivity and bondage in Babylon, God made this chilling summary statement of nearly ten centuries of Israel's history:

---

[14]Ex. 20:8, Num. 15:39–40, Deut. 4:10, 5:15, 7:18, 8:2, 18, 9:7, 11:2, 15:15, 16:3, 12, 24:9, 18, 22, 25:17, 32:7.

> Does a maiden forget her jewelry,
>   a bride her wedding ornaments?
> Yet my people have forgotten me,
>   days without number. (Jer. 2:32)

God says his people had forgotten him so many times that he had nearly lost track! Lest we quickly pass judgment on God's forgetting faithful, however, we must first admit that their malady is ours too. It is an unfortunate fact of life that, left to ourselves, we will all slowly squeeze God out of our thoughts and out of our lives. The previous chapter on Asaph is indisputable evidence of this. And just as Asaph, by forgetting God, lost sight of the value of righteousness, we too will lose perspective. We will lose sight of the value of the present and the prospects for the future.

Let's look at a few of the things that can cause us to forget God.

Prosperity: Means or End?

One of the greatest threats to our relationship with God is prosperity. Material or emotional security can easily become an end in itself, rather than a means to an end. God had called the Jews to become his people. In his own words, "Now if you obey me fully and keep my covenant, then out of all nations you will be my treasured possession." (Ex. 19:5). When Israel entered the Promised Land, they experienced material prosperity. But they quickly forgot that material prosperity was merely a sign of God's blessing, not an end in itself. They made the short but deadly migration from prosperity as blessing to prosperity as business.

The Lord knew this was going to happen. They were going to experience a transition from manna to meat loaf, from a tent in the wilderness to a home by the brook. The temptations to forget God would be enormous. And God sought to forewarn them as they stood outside the Promised Land, ready to enter:

Be careful that you do not forget the LORD your God, failing to observe his commands, his laws and his decrees that I am giving you this day. Otherwise, when you eat and are satisfied, when you build fine houses and settle down, and when your herds and flocks grow large and your silver and gold increase and all you have is multiplied, then your heart will become proud and you will forget the LORD your God, who brought you out of Egypt, out of the land of slavery. (Deut. 8:11–14)

God feared that Israel would become satisfied with what he *gave*, rather than with God himself. One of the reasons the Old Testament Jews "forgot God days without number" is because they looked at their prosperity in the present as an end in itself.

Pride: No Need for God?

A second cause of forgetting God is closely linked to, perhaps even a consequence of, the first. While prosperity can cause us to focus on the gift rather than the Giver, it can also slowly shift our sense of dependence from God to ourselves. It can lead to a sense of independence from God. The Lord warned infant Israel of this temptation as well:

You may say to yourself, "My power and the strength of my hands have produced this wealth for me." But remember the LORD your God, for it is he who gives you the ability to produce wealth. (Deut. 8:17–18)

Forgetting God is at the root of the myth of nostalgia. When we aim our sights on the events, people, and things of the past *apart from God,* the One who actually made the past possible, we lose sight of the larger truth that the past is nothing more than a record of God's dealings with us. It is not a time to long for, but rather a season to learn from. Paul gives us his own prescription for dealing with the past in his letter to the church at Philippi:

> But one thing I do: Forgetting what is behind and straining toward what is ahead, I press on toward the goal to win the prize for which God has called me heavenward in Christ Jesus. All of us who are mature should take such a view of things. (Phil. 3:13–15)

It has been said that the past should be a signpost, not a hitching post. This is especially true for the child of God. When we think of the past, we need to be sure that we remember *God and his dealings with us* in the past, never simply the things, people, or events in themselves.

The prophet Jeremiah was well-acquainted with the difficulty of maintaining a clear picture of the past in the face of an unpleasant present. His method of dealing with this problem is very insightful:

> I remember my affliction and my wandering,
>   the bitterness and the gall.
> I well remember them,
>   and my soul is downcast within me.
> Yet this I call to mind
>   and therefore I have hope:
>
> Because of the LORD's great love we are not consumed,
>   for his compassions never fail.
> They are new every morning;
>   great is your faithfulness. (Lam. 3:19–23)

Jeremiah was honest about the frustration, pain, and discouragement he was facing. His strength for the present came from a willful recollection of the past. But he did not muse on better days gone by. Rather, he meditated on the *character of God* that was behind those better days. Jeremiah reflected on God, not on what God had given.

Jill follows Jeremiah's example. She has a collection of more than twenty journals she has used to record her own spiritual pilgrimage and that of our family over the past two decades. While most of it is very private, periodically she will read some of it to me or to the whole family. It is so refreshing to get a balanced picture of the past and a reminder of where God has brought us. Every time she reads to us from it, the past becomes an encouragement in the present, not an era to envy and escape to.

The past is a beautiful provision of our gracious Father, in which we can see his careful and loving care. But if we are not careful, the "glass" through which we gaze becomes smudged and the picture distorted. If your view of the past makes your present circumstances unbearable or more difficult, maybe it is time to "clean the glass"!

EIGHT

Jeremiah: Looking for Success

Have little care that Life is brief
And less that Art is long.
Success is in the silences,
Though Fame is in the song.[15]

Few people really believe that "success is in the silences"—that genuine success is a quiet thing. Life tends to herd us in the opposite direction—toward notoriety, noise, and nonsense. We have been conditioned to view success as a flamboyant thing.

I know a middle-aged Christian husband and father who left a career in secondary education to pursue a dream—becoming a college professor. All his friends and his extended family were thrilled to see him get out of the "rat race" of teaching teenagers. The prospect of being on the college campus was quite appealing. He worked hard for two years to secure funding for the additional education.

---

[15]Bliss Carmen, *Songs From Vagabondia: Envoy*, quoted in Burton Stevenson, ed., *The Home Book of Quotations*, (New York: Greenwich House, 1984), 1928.

After a long and arduous process, he was awarded a tax-free fellowship for a doctoral program at a prestigious, nearby private college. It seemed as though his dreams were unfolding faster than he could imagine. It looked as though he would be able to provide for his children's college education at last. He envisioned himself embracing the security, prestige, and reasonable work hours he had longed for.

However, three months before he was to begin his doctoral studies, a gnawing sense of unrest began to grow in his heart. Slowly but certainly he became convinced that God wanted him to return to teaching high school, decline the fellowship, and bid farewell to his dreams.

If you had known this individual during his two-year ordeal, how would you have counseled him? Would you have become frustrated and even angry with his apparent lack of vision and motivation? Some of his friends did. They saw his choice as a foolish and irresponsible whim. "God doesn't lead us in circles!" one person told him.

Would you consider this man a success?

Tim Hansel comments on the increasing importance of one's *work* as a measure of success in our culture:

> In our culture, work has become one of the biggest factors in determining personal identity. It is not surprising, therefore, that work is often assigned universal and unqualified value. It becomes a basis for measuring human worth.[16]

In other words, *what* a person does has become the grounds for determining his or her worth. And it isn't just what we do, but how well we do it. It is no longer enough to be a doctor, lawyer, contractor, teacher, or homemaker. The question confronting all of us today is, How successful are we at what we do. Success has

---

[16]Tim Hansel,*When I Relax I Feel Guilty* (Elgin, Ill.: David C. Cook, 1979), 35.

become the credential for personal worth. The greater our success, the greater our value.

Nor is even success the real issue. Rather, the final arbiter of our value is what others perceive our success to be. *Image* is more important than substance.

Even though we'd like to be able to say that this utilitarian measure of worth dominates the world of careers but not the world of faith, Christians also tend to measure their value by their volume. Spiritual worth, for many, is determined by one's "usefulness" to God, or more bluntly, how successful one is in the "things of God." We all feel a vague sense of pressure to accomplish something "significant" for God in our lifetime. This pressure to produce translates into believing that unless we achieve something noticeable, measurable, and perhaps even enviable before we die, our lives will have been wasted.

This debilitating perspective is further accentuated by a second tendency among Christians regarding success: We tend to hold "high-profile" believers in greater esteem than the rest of us. People like Chuck Swindoll, Beverly LaHaye, Pat Robertson, and Chuck Colson are viewed as successful Christians because of their incredible breadth of impact. We tend to equate prominence and success, in ministry no less than in other areas of life.

The unfortunate byproduct of such a high view of others is a low view of ourselves. It is impossible to see ourselves as successful in comparison to Christians such as these. It is common for Christian men and women—especially those in mid-life—to conclude that they are of little value to God, themselves, or the world. When this happens, discouragement and depression are on the doorstep.

Why is it so easy to ascribe success to others and failure to ourselves? I believe it has to do with our misunderstanding of fame and success.

Our Distorted View of Fame and Success

We have turned fame into a cult. We have television shows about the lifestyles of the rich and famous; tabloids that promenade the famous before our eyes; and a host of other smorgasbords of celebrity cuisine to tease and titillate our secret passions. Even in the Christian world, as we have noted, the cult of celebrity has found a home. "Big name" Christians are sought after like rock stars to adorn the ads for Christian concerts, cruises, and conferences. The church is playing the "fame game" as well as the world.

Thomas Fuller said that, "Fame is a magnifying glass."[17] A magnifying glass does at least two things that illustrate the dangers inherent in our distorted view of fame.

First of all, a magnifying glass exaggerates the size of things; it makes objects appear bigger than they actually are. Famous people become "bigger than life" to us. They take on a special aura of intellect, ability, joy, and self-esteem. We are enchanted with this exaggerated view. Unfortunately, this is as true of our view of celebrated Christians as it is of those represented by the stars imbedded in the sidewalks of Hollywood. We have come to believe that "famous" Christians don't struggle with the same things we do; or that somehow they have progressed beyond the daily grind that characterizes so much of our own existence.

Another thing a magnifying glass does—by virtue of its own limitations—is only show *part* of an object. Fame, like a magnifying glass, provides a restricted picture. We are only allowed to see a very small portion of the person's life and character—the part that has made them famous. We mistakenly assume that this tiny fragment is representative of the person as a whole.

In the world of Christian stardom, this translates into expectations of perfection. We can actually believe some Christians have

---

[17]Thomas Fuller, Gnomologia, quoted in Burton Stevenson, ed., The Home Book of Quotations, (New York: Greenwich House, 1984), 623.

done away with their sin natures in their rise to holy fame. We are shocked and outraged when they suddenly announce that they are getting divorced, or when they are found guilty of embezzlement and fraud. There are certainly biblical grounds for high expectations of those in leadership, but we must be careful to determine how much of our "outrage" is due to our own illusions from looking through the magnifying glass of fame.

A second reason we are so quick to ascribe success to others and failure to ourselves is that we fail to understand what comprises genuine success. And if we hold an inaccurate view of success it is likely, perhaps even certain, that we will be failures in our own eyes.

God has preserved in the pages of Scripture the account of a young, struggling preacher who by American standards would have been forced to resign shortly after he began his ministry. In the life of Jeremiah, the "Weeping Prophet," we see in vivid detail not only an example of true, godly success, but also the stark contrast between genuine success and mere fame.

Background on the Prophet

While we are not certain of the exact age at which Jeremiah was called to the ministry, we can assume from his own dialogue with God that he was considered "young" for the assignment:

The word of the LORD came to me, saying,

"Before I formed you in the womb I knew you,
    before you were born I set you apart;
I appointed you as a prophet to the nations."

"Ah, Sovereign LORD," I said, "I do not know how to speak; I am only a child." (Jer. 1:4–6)

While we cannot pinpoint Jeremiah's exact age, we can determine when his ministry began and how long it lasted. In the second verse of the first chapter we are told, "The word of the LORD came to him in the thirteenth year of the reign of Josiah son of Amon king of Judah." This was 626 B.C. We also know that Jeremiah's ministry lasted at least until the temple in Jerusalem was destroyed in 586 B.C. That means his prophetic ministry extended over a period of at least forty years. The great length of Jeremiah's ministry will become significant as we consider the meaning of true success.

Jeremiah was commissioned to preach to the Jews of the southern kingdom (Judah), demanding that they repent of their wickedness lest God punish them just as he had punished the northern kingdom (Israel) nearly 150 years earlier (see 2 Kings 17). During the reign of Rehoboam, the son of Solomon and grandson of King David, the nation of Israel had split into two kingdoms, each with its own capital city. God had warned the wayward and unfaithful northern kingdom through the ministry of the prophet Isaiah, but they had not listened. Consequently, God sent Sennacherib, king of Assyria, to conquer and destroy the northern kingdom (2 Kings 18:10). Sennacherib deported the Jews to Assyria and imported Gentiles to live in the land once occupied by God's people. The intermarriages that eventually took place gave rise to the Samaritans—the half-breeds so despised by the Jews of Jesus' day.

Jeremiah appears on the scene nearly a century-and-a-half later to warn the southern kingdom that the fate of their relatives to the north awaited them as well.

How effective was Jeremiah's preaching? Suffice it to say that Jerusalem was sacked, the temple was totally destroyed by the Babylonians, and the Jews were deported to Babylon as captives in 586 B.C. Let's take a closer look at Jeremiah's "resumé" and evaluate his relative success in the ministry.

Fame or Infamy?

It came as no surprise to Jeremiah that he was not the most sought after preacher in the district. God had warned him from the very beginning that he would be intensely unpopular because of his message:

> "I will pronounce my judgments on my people
>   because of their wickedness in forsaking me,
> in burning incense to other gods
>   and in worshiping what their hands have made.

> "Get yourself ready! Stand up and say to them whatever I command you. Do not be terrified by them, or I will terrify you before them. Today I have made you a fortified city, an iron pillar and a bronze wall to stand against the whole land—against the kings of Judah, its officials, its priests and the people of the land. They will fight against you but will not overcome you, for I am with you and will rescue you," declares the LORD. (Jer. 1:16–19)

Indeed, the opposition God had predicted materialized in short order. Jeremiah was arrested, beaten, put in stocks, and held up to public ridicule (20:1–2). In fact, Jeremiah tells us that insult and ridicule were his daily diet: "I am ridiculed all day long; everyone mocks me" (20:7). When God commanded him to tell the people that surrender to the Babylonians was their only hope, the hostility against the prophet grew to such proportions that many of the spiritual leaders demanded his immediate death. He was "exiled" to an empty cistern: "They lowered Jeremiah by ropes into the cistern; it had no water in it, only mud, and Jeremiah sank down into the mud" (38:6). One has to wonder if Jeremiah's condition in the cistern is also a caricature of the larger picture of what was happening to his emotional and spiritual health—"sinking down into the mud"!

While it is obvious that there was opposition to his message, the record also reveals that Jeremiah himself was rejected by many if not most of the significant people in his life. People from his hometown of Anathoth, likely his own neighbors, sought to kill him (11:19–21). The members of his immediate family rejected him and what he had to say (12:6). Those in positions of spiritual leadership, the priests and other prophets, considered him a dangerous nuisance. They even had a nickname for him: "Terror on every side"! (20:10) The king rejected Jeremiah, and mocked him by shredding and burning the scroll that contained his message (36:23). Finally, we learn in 26:8 that Jeremiah was rejected by the general public: "But as soon as Jeremiah finished telling all the people everything the LORD had commanded him to say, the priests, the prophets and all the people seized him and said, 'You must die!'"

At this point Jeremiah is surely the epitome of failure. A man who is hated and rejected by those in authority, those in a position to authenticate his worth. Even his own family has turned on him!

And there's no question that Jeremiah was adversely affected by all this failure:

> Cursed be the day I was born!
>   May the day my mother bore me not be blessed!
> Cursed be the man who brought my father the news,
>   who made him very glad, saying,
>   "A child is born to you—a son!"
> May that man be like the towns
>   the LORD overthrew without pity.
> May he hear wailing in the morning,
>   a battle cry at noon.
> For he did not kill me in the womb,
>   with my mother as my grave,
>   her womb enlarged forever.
> Why did I ever come out of the womb
>   to see trouble and sorrow
>   and to end my days in shame? (Jer. 20:14–18)

Make no mistake, Jeremiah is depressed! Wouldn't you be? And we know that his depression did not leave him quickly. It was much more than a "mood swing." Its intensity still lingers as he recollects it in writing his "memoirs" on the whole matter—the book of Lamentations:

> I became the laughingstock of all my people;
>   they mock me in song all day long.
> He has filled me with bitter herbs
>   and sated me with gall.
> He has broken my teeth with gravel;
>   he has trampled me in the dust.
> I have been deprived of peace;
>   I have forgotten what prosperity is.
> So I say, "My splendor is gone
>   and all that I had hoped from the LORD."
>
> I remember my affliction and my wandering,
>   the bitterness and the gall.
> I well remember them,
>   and my soul is downcast within me. (Lam. 3:14–20)

These are the honest comments of a man who has embraced failure as a bosom friend. Success has eluded him at every turn. His "splendor is gone and all that [he] had hoped for from the Lord." Jeremiah had seen absolutely no response in the hearts or lives of his own countrymen *in over forty years of faithful preaching!* Not only had his efforts been of no avail, but he had lost any notoriety he had in the process. If one's worth is truly a product of their cumulative success in the eyes of significant others, this man's life was a waste.

But was it? Was Jeremiah a failure or a success? What was the "bottom line" for this prophet? What kept him going in the midst of opposition and rejection. And more importantly, when it was all over, how did Jeremiah *see himself*?

Results, Rewards, or Relationship?

Jeremiah did not witness any tangible "results" from his faithful preaching of God's message. So, in truth, he "accomplished" nothing for God that God couldn't have done without him. As Jeremiah began his ministry, God warned the Jews that Jerusalem would be destroyed and the people would be taken captive. Forty years later, that's exactly what happened. All Jeremiah's preaching didn't change a thing. It could be argued that his ministry was a failure—especially by current standards of judging a ministry's success.

But Jeremiah didn't see it that way. While the pain of his past and the destruction of his city were still vivid memories, Jeremiah didn't measure his worth by what he had *accomplished* for God. As we saw in the last chapter, his focus was someplace else:

> I remember my affliction and my wandering,
>   the bitterness and the gall.
> I well remember them,
>   and my soul is downcast within me.
> Yet this I call to mind
>   and therefore I have hope:
>
> Because of the LORD's great love
>   we are not consumed,
>   for his compassions never fail.
> They are new every morning;
>   great is your faithfulness.
> I say to myself, "The LORD is my portion;
>   therefore I will wait for him." (Lam. 3:19–24)

Jeremiah said that his "reward" or inheritance from forty years of fruitless yet faithful service was *the Lord himself*! Jeremiah reveled in his relationship with God, not in the results of or rewards from his own preaching. This idea is so foreign to us, it is almost offensive. We who are accustomed and addicted to the accolades of others will find it difficult to view a deeper relationship with God as the "reward" for our efforts.

It is interesting to note that the prophets who were "successful" with the people of Jeremiah's day were very unsavory to God:

> "A horrible and shocking thing
>   has happened in the land:
> The prophets prophesy lies,
>   the priests rule by their own authority,
>   and my people love it this way.
> But what will you do in the end?" (Jer. 5:30–31)

Even though they may have secured all the TV specials, radio interviews, publishing agreements, and megachurches, these prophets were all on God's "black list" because they were obsessed with success rather than with something more important.

Those of us who claim to operate according to the economy of God's kingdom should never view success in terms of how many, how big, or how much. We should never measure it by results. Jeremiah stands forever as a testimony to what constitutes genuine success—something well within the reach of every Christian.

Success God's Way

The only claim Jeremiah could make was that he had done precisely what God had asked. The Lord never told Jeremiah to save the nation, preserve the temple, or initiate a reformation of national proportions. God had asked Jeremiah to preach to an unrepentant nation, and then told him precisely what to preach. Jeremiah did what was asked. Jeremiah *succeeded*, because he completed his assigned task. We think that "serving" God involves intense involvement in religious activities or causes. The sobering truth is, unless God has *asked* us to do something, we are not serving him by doing it. It is a foolish notion to believe that a servant chooses the terms of his service.

The implications of this are staggering. It may actually be more spiritual to say no to certain ministry opportunities than to say yes! If God has not asked you or me to do something, then doing it is not serving him, regardless of how zealously or how well we do it.

If genuine service to God merely involves obedience to the task he assigns, then Jeremiah couldn't have been more obedient, or more successful. To God, faithfulness always has priority over fruitfulness:

> With what shall I come before the LORD
>   and bow down before the exalted God?
> Shall I come before him with burnt offerings,
>   with calves a year old?
> Will the LORD be pleased with thousands of rams,
>   with ten thousand rivers of oil?
> Shall I offer my firstborn for my transgression,
>   the fruit of my body for the sin of my soul?
> He has showed you, O man, what is good.
>   And what does the LORD require of you?
> To act justly and to love mercy
>   and to walk humbly with your God. (Mic. 6:6–8)

Doing what God asks is our responsibility. Changing the world is his. When we reverse those responsibilities, we are adopting the world's standards for success.

Seek to Finish

The life of the apostle Paul is an excellent illustration of the principles embodied in Jeremiah's ministry. Although Paul experienced sensational success in his ministry—the opposite of Jeremiah—his focus was identical to Jeremiah's:

However, I consider my life worth nothing to me, if only I may finish the race and complete the task the Lord Jesus has given me—the task of testifying to the gospel of God's grace. (Acts 20:24)

For I am already being poured out like a drink offering, and the time has come for my departure. I have fought the good fight, I have finished the race, I have kept the faith. (2 Tim. 4:6–7)

Early in his life (the above passage from Acts) Paul said the only thing he wanted to do was to "finish the race" of obedience. He said nothing about *winning* the race, of being the best apostle, the most influential, or the most esteemed. He spoke only of "finishing." Then, at the end of his life and ministry (the passage from 2 Timothy), he boasts that he had indeed "finished the race." Paul had set his heart on the finish, not on fame. You cannot have it both ways.

The lives of Jeremiah and Paul are beautiful illustrations of true success—men who sought the finish line rather than the spotlight. We must seek first to *finish*, not to be famous. We need to make choices today that will ensure that we are still walking with God tomorrow. Fame is a magnifying glass. It affords us the luxury of the short-view, but sacrifices the ultimate on the altar of the immediate. If I set my sights on finishing the race rather than on the winner's circle, I will pace myself to that end. I doubt that God is genuinely glorified by those who "do great things" for him early on, and then drop out of the race in their later years. In fact, we should take great care that we don't contribute to making Christian leaders into celebrities early in life . . . and in so doing encourage them toward fame rather than toward the finish line.

Do you remember our high school teacher who said no to opportunity and advancement at the opening of this chapter? Does God always lead in straight lines? Does God's path for his children always ascend to greater heights of notoriety, salary, and security? If so, this man was and is a failure. Somehow, though, I'm not prepared to call my friend a failure. One reason is that my friend is

myself! But a more significant reason is that God's measure of success has to do only with our fidelity. Being faithful to what *he*
asks—and being faithful to the end—makes any man or woman a
success in the eyes of God.

NINE

Job:
When the Lights Go Out

The depression that resulted from Elijah's fatigue, Moses' failure to delegate, and (as we shall see in chapter 11) Jonah's self-centeredness, all had one thing in common—it was within the control of those who experienced it. Sometimes, however, we can find ourselves immersed in a discouragement that is beyond our control, and one for which we cannot totally be blamed. Sometimes our most painful trials of faith, during which we are tempted to despair, are due to a deliberate silence on the part of God.

Such was the case with Job. The occasion for Job's depression was not things within his control, indeed it was not even within the control of other human beings. Job became deeply depressed as a result of excruciating circumstances that can be traced directly back to God himself. This kind of suffering is the most difficult, because it not only causes us intense pain, but also tempts us to doubt the goodness and love of God. And without a deep conviction of God's presence in the midst of suffering, life quickly becomes meaningless and cruel—the two conclusions at which Job eventually arrived.

The book of Job contains very little about the actual circumstances that induced Job's depression. In fact, of the forty-two chapters in the book, only the first two deal with what happened to him. The rest is a record of Job's own comments about his situation, or the dialogue that occurred between him and his four "counselors."

Job's opening comments are prefaced by these words: "After this, Job opened his mouth and cursed the day of his birth" (Job 3:1). As the main section of the book commences, the man is already so depressed he wishes he had never been born! He goes on in graphic terms to describe his own circumstances and feelings:

> "For sighing comes to me instead of food;
>   my groans pour out like water.
> What I feared has come upon me;
>   what I dreaded has happened to me.
> I have no peace, no quietness;
>   I have no rest, but only turmoil." (3:24–26)

This suffocating atmosphere of despair and despondency permeates every page of the book. The pain and suffering God brought into Job's life was of a magnitude perhaps unparalleled in Scripture, except of course for that of our Lord. Unfortunately, Job's suffering that led him to despair was also due, in a large part, to the fruitless and often flawed counsel of his "friends."

In this chapter we'll examine Job and his responses to the painful ordeal God asked him to endure. From that we can glean some vital principles for ourselves when confronting similar difficulties. But we also want to study Job's friends, particularly their comments and methods in trying to help Job. They provide us with a wealth of examples of how *not* to help a friend in a crisis.

Background on the Man

The first two chapters of Job are rich with insights into Job's life and personality. From the book's opening lines, we discover that he was a man of sterling character and great wealth:

> In the land of Uz there lived a man whose name was Job. This man was blameless and upright; he feared God and shunned evil. He had seven sons and three daughters, and he owned seven thousand sheep, three thousand camels, five hundred yoke of oxen and five hundred donkeys, and had a large number of servants. He was the greatest man among all the people of the East. (1:1–3)

Job was "blameless and upright." He loved God and wanted to make sure that his own life was pleasing to him. But he also wanted to see this personal holiness reflected in the other members of his family. We learn in these early verses that he regularly prayed for his children's spiritual welfare.

We can also surmise from these opening verses that Job had a great deal of wealth and owned enormous areas of land—to sustain such large flocks and herds. The cumulative effect of owning huge parcels of land, livestock, and servants . . . is power. Job was undoubtedly a very powerful man in the land of Uz. The description, "He was the greatest man among all the people of the East" must be understood in terms of both wealth and power. And Job's prestige, power, and influence came from his assets more than from his character. Job was respected for his character . . . but his power came from his wealth.

Socially, Job was well-known. We are told that he "instructed many" and "strengthened feeble hands" (4:3). He was a person others came to in time of need. He must have been a man of wide reputation and sound counsel. He was the sort of person you would seek out if you had a problem. This social status is even more clearly stated later on in the book:

"When I went to the gate of the city
  and took my seat in the public square,
the young men saw me and stepped aside
  and the old men rose to their feet;
the chief men refrained from speaking
  and covered their mouths with their hands;
the voices of the nobles were hushed,
  and their tongues stuck to the roof of their mouths.
Whoever heard me spoke well of me,
  and those who saw me commended me." (29:7–11)

Job was a well-thought-of, highly respected leader in the land
of Uz.

Job's Circumstances Revisited

One of the most vital facts in this entire story is that the
tragedies which befell Job can be traced back to *God*, not to Satan.
While it is true that Satan was the immediate cause of Job's trials, he
was not the instigator—God was! It was God, not Satan who
dragged Job's name into the discussion:

The LORD said to Satan, "Where have you come from?"
  Satan answered the LORD, "From roaming through the earth and
going back and forth in it."
  Then the LORD said to Satan, "Have you considered my servant
Job? There is no one on earth like him; he is blameless and upright,
a man who fears God and shuns evil." (1:6–8)

God was responsible for Job's trials! The suffering Job was called
to endure and conquer came by the hand of Satan, but it also came
from the heart of God.

God was well-acquainted with the Devil. He knew that as soon
as he introduced Job into the discussion, Satan would want
to destroy him. Satan is called the "accuser of our brothers"

(Rev. 12:10), and indeed that is just what he did to Job. He "accused" him of being faithful to God, not because he loved him, but rather because he loved what God had done for him. God said, "Job loves *me*," and Satan said, "Job loves the *benefits* of knowing you."

God then gave Satan the opportunity to prove his accusation. And I believe the reason God gave Satan such liberty in Job's life was because he knew that Job would not fail. In fact, the Lord knew that Job would emerge a stronger and more faithful servant of God. Difficult circumstances are never intended by God merely to "push us over the edge." God's desire and plan with us today, as with Job, is always to purify our faith and deepen our love. In the process of allowing Satan the liberty to try to prove his accusations against the children of God, the Lord is glorified and Satan humiliated in the sight of the heavenly hosts. Angels are not omniscient. They can actually learn about God by observing our lives—especially how we respond to suffering and pain. I believe that is at least part of the meaning in Paul's statement:

> His intent was that now, through the church, the manifold wisdom of God should be made known to the rulers and authorities in the heavenly realms, according to his eternal purpose which he accomplished in Christ Jesus our Lord. (Eph. 3:10–11)

So, God gives Satan limited liberty to attack Job. He is not allowed to touch *him*, only the things that are important to him. And much like a small child who is given a parental restriction, Satan pushes God's permission to the very limits; he does everything he possibly can to show God and the heavenly hosts that Job doesn't love God. And the easiest and quickest way to do that is to remove the blessings of God, in hopes that our feelings for God will evaporate. When there are no feelings *of* love and no benefits *to* love, only genuine love will abide.

Satan sets out to systematically unravel the very fabric of Job's existence. First, Job loses all of his oxen and donkeys and the servants tending them, to a raiding band of Sabeans (1:13–15). Then, his sheep and their shepherds are destroyed by a natural disaster (v. 16). Next, his camels are stolen by three raiding parties of Chaldeans, and the servants with them are killed. Finally, a windstorm arises suddenly and strikes the house where his children are celebrating, killing his seven sons and three daughters. Job's entire life is destroyed in a few hours' time!

The account of this tragic day in Job's life in chapter 1 makes it clear that the news of these four catastrophes reached Job one at a time. Suffering that arrives in "waves" is more relentless in its attack than that which announces itself all at once. Satan knew that and employed it boldly with Job.

In a single day this prince was reduced to a pauper. Job's financial holdings were completely wiped out. It was the equivalent of Donald Trump going broke in a single day! In Job's time, there was no such thing as insurance. The closest thing one had to protection against this type of calamity was a large family, particularly many sons, and Job was robbed of even that security. He was left facing the stark reality that not only had he lost all the emblems of earthly success, but there was no way he could ever recover them.

Job's response to all this was extreme grief and despondency, enveloped in genuine worship:

> At this, Job got up and tore his robe and shaved his head. Then he fell to the ground in worship and said:
>
> "Naked I came from my mother's womb,
>   and naked I will depart.
> The LORD gave and the LORD has taken away;
>   may the name of the LORD be praised."
>
> In all this, Job did not sin by charging God with wrongdoing. (1:20–22)

Job's worship is evident in his acknowledgment that everything he had, including his children, was an endowment from God. How could he be bitter for losing something that was a gift in the first place? We must be careful however, not to conclude that the statement that Job *did* not "charge God with wrongdoing" means that Job didn't attribute his circumstances to the hand of God. It is clear from the rest of the book that Job did charge God with what had happened; but he did *not* charge God with wrongdoing. Job knew that what had come into his life was either by the direct wishes of God or at least within the perimeter of his permissive will. He saw God as the cause, yet did not attribute blame. This is the response of godly maturity. Job wept. Job grieved. But then Job worshiped. Too often, we cannot get beyond the first two; we end up charging God with wrongdoing, which is sin. But Job didn't. He withstood Satan's attempt to prove that his devotion was mere sentiment, the fruit of a comfortable life.

Unfortunately, God was not yet finished with Job.

God initiates a second conversation with Satan on the subject of Job. It is in this subsequent conversation that we learn with certainty that Job had done nothing to "earn" these trials:

> Then the Lord said to Satan, "Have you considered my servant Job? There is no one on earth like him; he is blameless and upright, a man who fears God and shuns evil. And he still maintains his integrity, though you incited me against him to ruin him without any reason." (2:3)

God knew precisely what Satan's response would be:

> "Skin for skin! . . . A man will give all he has for his own life. But stretch out your hand and strike his flesh and bones, and he will surely curse you to your face." (2:4–5)

By once again drawing attention to Job, God is also pointing out Satan's failure to break him. And because pride is the driving force in Satan's corrupted nature, he demands a second chance, with higher stakes. So God gives his Enemy permission to strike Job's health, as long as he spares his life. And Satan quickly and gladly exploits this liberty by striking Job with a skin disorder that produces open sores from the "soles of his feet to the top of his head." (2:7)

But Satan is not allowed to take Job's life. Job's wife wanted him to die (2:9); Job himself wanted to die (3:1); and Satan would have loved to kill him. It appears that the only person who wanted to keep Job alive was God. Even in the midst of tragedy and hardship, we are called to live for the praise of God's glory.

Job's wife typifies the common human tendency to be impatient with the suffering of others. She belittles Job's perseverance: "Are you still holding on to your integrity? Curse God and die!" (2:9) Remember: Job's wife has nothing to gain by his death in terms of wealth and property. He lost all of that in Satan's initial onslaught. There can only be one reason why she is eager for him to die—she is weary of caring for him and listening to his tale of woe. He has become a burden to her. When we realize that God wanted Job to live, we also see that Job's wife was missing the will of God for her own life. There was something in all of this for her as well as for Job. It is common for us to overlook the very real probability that God has us in mind too, when he brings a trial upon someone we love. And his plans for us involve more than the basic necessity of being a care-giver. Job's wife failed to see the larger picture of the sovereignty of God. Job tried to remind her of that in his response to her cutting remark: "You are talking like a foolish woman. Shall we accept good from God, and not trouble?" (v. 10)

We also learn that Satan's real target was God himself. He cared nothing for Job. Satan wanted to humiliate *God*, by getting Job to "curse him to his face." His goals and strategies have not changed. We too are of little consequence to Satan. He undoubtedly enjoys seeing people suffer, but our suffering means nothing to him if it does not bring us to the place where we will charge God with wrongdoing. God is always Satan's target. We are little more than a disposable means to that end. Our perseverance in suffering is a legitimate way to hold up the name of God in the face of his enemy and ours.

Satan's goals are clear. But what about God's? What was he hoping to accomplish in the life of Job? Why, in the words of a recent book title, do "bad things happen to good people"? Obtaining a satisfactory answer to these questions is essential to understanding and coping with the depression that usually follows a deliberate silence on the part of God.

Why Did Job Suffer?

After the first two chapters, where we are introduced to the causes of his suffering, the remainder of the book of Job consists of dialogues between Job and his four friends, and concludes with a conversation between Job and the Lord.

The first person to respond to Job's grief is Eliphaz. His diagnosis is simply that Job is suffering because of his sin:

> "Consider now: Who, being innocent, has ever perished?
>   Where were the upright ever destroyed?
> As I have observed,
>   those who plow evil and those who sow trouble reap it. . . .
>
> "Can a mortal be more righteous than God?
>   Can a man be more pure than his Maker?" (4:7–8, 17)

In other words, says Eliphaz, Job is reaping what he has sown. Job's suffering is his own fault. And because of that, he should quit complaining and "face the music."

Bildad, the second "counselor" provides a slight variation on the theme begun by Eliphaz. He stresses the principle of cause and effect:

"When your children sinned against him,
    he gave them over to the penalty of their sin. . . .

"Can papyrus grow tall where there is no marsh?
    Can reeds thrive without water? . . .

"While still growing and uncut,
    they wither more quickly than grass.
Such is the destiny of all who forget God;
    so perishes the hope of the godless." (8:4, 11–13)

Bildad says that all effects demand a cause, and suffering is the consequence of forgetting God. Sin is the cause of pain and death. Job's children died, therefore they must have sinned. Job himself is in great anguish; obviously he too must have sinned.

Next, Zophar appears in chapter 11 with his own conclusions. First he condemns Job's complaints as the idle chatter of an arrogant and mocking man, then he tells Job that what he is experiencing is *less* than what he actually deserves! "Know this: God has even forgotten some of your sin." (11:6)

Finally the youngest of the four, Elihu, blurts out:

"I am young in years, and you are old;
that is why I was fearful,
    not daring to tell you what I know.
I thought, 'Age should speak;
    advanced years should teach wisdom.'" (32:6–7)

Elihu's ensuing comments, which fill the next six chapters, are typical of those who have lived little. His experience and knowledge of God are limited, and it shows. Elihu not only rebukes Job as an arrogant and unrighteous man. He also chides the other three for their apparent ignorance. As is always the case with those whose intersections with human pain are few, Elihu sees Job's circumstances as a black-and-white issue, obvious to any discerning mind. And of course he, too, misses the bigger picture due to his preoccupation with what he sees.

All of these men conclude in one fashion or another that there is a simple and clear cause for Job's pain: sin. *His* sin. Were they correct? Was Job suffering for his own sin, the fruit of ungodly choices? There *are* times when sin elicits the discipline of God. Paul tells us in 1 Corinthians 11:27–30 that there was a direct relationship between unconfessed sin, and the sickness and death in the church at Corinth. It is obviously possible for our sin to have serious, even tragic consequences. But there is no indication that this was the case with Job. In fact just the opposite was true. God called him "blameless and upright," both before and after Satan's first attack on him. (1:8, 2:3)

I wrote this particular chapter because of an extended time of depression in my own life. For two years it was as if God had gone on vacation. I sought earnestly to make sense out of his silence, and out of the Christian life in general. I searched every nook and corner of my soul for some sin that might have offended God and sent him away.

Of course I found a host of things that seemed significant enough to explain God's silence. That was to be expected. My sin nature, like yours, is a constant foe this side of eternity. But I slowly began to see, from my study of Job's life, that God had not gone anywhere because of my transgressions. He was not responding to my sin. He merely wanted me to know that one of the truest evidences of love for him is the willingness to walk in the dark as well as in the light:

> Who among you fears the LORD
>   and obeys the word of his servant?
> Let him who walks in the dark,

who has no light,
trust in the name of the LORD
and rely on his God. (Isa. 50:10)

I, like Job, was learning that our following God sometimes happens best when there is no *awareness* of his presence, only the *assurance* of it.

We, like Job's friends, tend to want to tell people why they are immersed in a trial. We are always looking for the "purpose" in pain. We are convinced that if we can just get an answer to the question, Why? we will be able to accept our own trials or explain someone else's. Of course we normally couch these analyses in spiritually embellished language such as, "I wonder if the Lord is trying to teach you such and such . . ." or, "Someday you'll really see why all of this happened." But secretly, we tend to think to ourselves, "If I were God, this is just what I would do to get their attention or develop a certain character quality in their life." Instead of honestly trying to understand the person's perspective and empathize with their pain, we put ourselves in the place of God as we omnisciently explain the reason for their suffering.

One of my high school students had chosen a path of obvious rebellion during her sophomore year. She was involved in two tragic accidents one after the other and ended up in double traction in the hospital. A well-meaning adult came to visit her. Following the example of Job's friends, he left her a pamphlet on the subject of "God's chastening"! In presuming to know the mind of God in regard to this young woman, he committed the same error that Job's friends did—speaking on God's behalf when God hadn't spoken to him. And in doing so, he drove this poor girl further into her misery, and farther from God.

The Urge To Say Something Profound

We can all-too-easily feel a tremendous pressure to say something profound in the face of suffering, pain, and death. Job suffered nearly as much at the hands of his so-called friends as he did from the wiles of Satan. We too can unwittingly become agents of destruction rather than of healing when we try to provide a why, where God hasn't. One of the most obvious principles from the life of Job is that we should remain silent in regard to the why of suffering in the lives of those we love.

The wife of one of my seminary professors died a slow, painful death from cancer. When she finally died, an unthinking Christian walked up to her husband and said, "What a blessing that she's gone to be with the Lord." While it is certainly true that her present state was preferable to the suffering, that comment totally neglected her husband's feelings. G. Campbell Morgan said that silence always gives grief a chance to express itself. The most compassionate thing Job's friends did was to remain quiet the first week they were with him. When they did that, Job felt the liberty to pour out his soul. And as chapter 3 opens, we find him sharing his bitterness, anguish, and pain with those who had come to console him. Unfortunately, rather than draw out his feeling further, they sought to show him the errors in his heart. When they sought to explain to Job the reason for his suffering, they began to fail both him and God. The story of Job is as much a documentation of how *not* to minister to those who are depressed as it is how to handle our own depression.

TEN

Job:
Walking in Darkness

Job's assessment of the ministry of his so-called friends is summarized in his statement,

> "I have heard many things like these;
>   miserable comforters are you all!
> Will your long-winded speeches never end?
>   What ails you that you keep on arguing?
> I also could speak like you, if you were in my place;
> I could make fine speeches against you
>   and shake my head at you.
> But my mouth would encourage you;
>   comfort from my lips would bring you relief." (Job 16:1–5)

Job's friends had brought him misery instead of ministry, heartache instead of healing. We have considered some of the causes of their failure as counselors. But their greatest failure was their failure to see the true nature of Job's suffering.

While it is certainly true that Job suffered immense physical pain from his own illness, and immeasurable emotional pain from the loss of his ten children, his deepest suffering came from a different source—the absence of God in Job's experience. From the very beginning of Job's trial, he makes it clear that this is the cause of his deepest struggle: "Why is life given to a man whose way is hidden, whom God has hedged in?" (3:23)

Not only is Job unable to see what is ahead for him, he is also unable to understand what is going on around him. He is boxed in, and the Lord is not in the box with him. And if God is not with him, then life is not worth living. He believes that even if he were to call for God and God were to come, he would not listen to what Job had to say (9:16). But the clearest statement regarding Job's spiritual vacuum is in 23:1–10:

Then Job replied:

"Even today my complaint is bitter;
    his hand is heavy in spite of my groaning.
If only I knew where to find him;
    if only I could go to his dwelling!
I would state my case before him
    and fill my mouth with arguments.
I would find out what he would answer me,
    and consider what he would say.
Would he oppose me with great power?
    No, he would not press charges against me.
There an upright man could present his case before him,
    and I would be delivered forever from my judge.

"But if I go to the east, he is not there;
    if I go to the west, I do not find him.
When he is at work in the north, I do not see him;
    when he turns to the south, I catch no glimpse of him.
But he knows the way that I take;
    when he has tested me, I will come forth as gold."

Job says that if he could just find God, things would be better. He believes that God is able to deliver him from his pain and suffering . . . if only he could find him. Instead, God is strangely absent from Job's experience. Job is alone in his pain. While Job still gives mental assent to God's existence ("when he has tested me, I will come forth as gold"), he cannot see God in the midst of his present circumstances. Job cannot locate a reference point, an anchor in the storm.

Is it true that God was not in the places where Job had looked? We know that the doctrine of God's omnipresence demands the recognition that God is everywhere. Yet Job was convinced that God had "hidden" himself from him. And it was this spiritual vacuum that produced Job's most severe pain. God had withheld the awareness of his presence from Job, and in so doing, Job was forced to face his circumstances and now his friends' accusations alone. He still had the conviction that God was real, but it was nothing more than mental assent to a biblical truth. He continued to pray, but was convinced that his prayers went no further than his ceiling. He continued to wait for God, but it looked more and more certain each day that God was not going to "show." And this was surely the most crushing aspect of Job's trial, smothered deep beneath the visible circumstances and pain. G. Campbell Morgan highlights this magnificently when he says:

> The very shock and surprise of the strokes create strength in which men triumph. It is in the brooding silence which enwraps the soul afterward that the fiercest fight is waged.[18]

Morgan captures the essence of Job's real battle. He had coped with the loss of all that was dear to him, including his family, his possessions, his own health, and the support of his wife. But then, in the week that followed, he silently pondered the circumstances that had ravaged his life. And in that period, he could not connect with God. Job's spiritual experience went dry in the midst of an already severe emotional drought. He had been accustomed to sweet daily fellowship with God. But now, when Job sought to

---

[18]G. Campbell Morgan, *An Exposition of the Whole Bible* (Old Tappan, N. J.: Revell, 1959), 202.

commune with God, it seemed that he was no longer present. Job was alone. It would be much like calling "911" in a crisis, only to get a recording that says, "We're sorry, that number has been disconnected."

Job's experience was by no means unique. Many of us find ourselves in similar circumstances today. Our prayer life seems like a monologue; our devotional times are dry and uninspiring. God's Word appears irrelevant or meaningless. Our joy has been replaced by apathy; our enthusiasm by indifference. God has gone on vacation, or so it seems. We, like Job, are alone in our experience.

Such emptiness is discouraging enough when life is easy. But it quickly becomes unbearable when times are difficult. It is understandable that Job was depressed. It is understandable that we become depressed in similar circumstances. But how does one face the silence of God? What should we do when God deliberately withholds an awareness of his presence in our experience?[19]

When God Is Silent

When God has hidden himself from our experience, whether it is in pain or in the routine of daily life, the very best thing we can do is the same thing other children of God have done—talk to ourselves! When the "lights have gone out," we need to keep telling ourselves of the truth. D. Martyn Lloyd-Jones, in his 1965 classic, *Spiritual Depression: Its Causes and Cure*, says:

> The whole danger is that when the mood comes upon us, we allow it to dominate us and we are defeated and depressed. We say that we would like to be delivered, and yet we do nothing about it. . . .
>   You have to speak to yourself. I have said this many times before and I shall go on saying it, for there is a sense in which what the

[19]For other instances where God "hid" himself, see Ps. 10:1, 13:1, Isa. 45:15, 50:10, Luke 24:15–17.

Scriptures do is to teach us how to speak to ourselves. . . . Remind yourself of certain things. Remind yourself of who you are and what you are. You must talk to yourself and say: "I am not going to be dominated by you, these moods shall not control me. I am going out, I am breaking through." . . .

I cannot make myself happy, but I can remind myself of my belief. I can exhort myself to believe, I can address my soul as the Psalmist did. . . . [I can] say, "No, I do not feel anything, but whether I feel or not, I believe the Scriptures. I believe God's Word is true and I will stay my soul on it, I will believe in it come what may."[20]

This "talking to yourself" is not to be confused with the modern notion of cognitive therapy, which has "feeling good" as one of its primary goals. Lloyd-Jones is simply suggesting that there are times when our feelings need to take the "back seat" to the revealed truth of God. In the case of Job, God was there even if Job could not feel him. The same is true when we struggle today. The biblical promise, "Never will I leave you; never will I forsake you" (Heb. 13:5), is true even when we feel forsaken by God and by others.

This promise is not dependent upon our own faithfulness. It is rooted in the unchangeable nature of God himself. It is impossible for him to desert us, even though he may remove our *awareness* of his presence.

The idea of talking to ourselves about the truth is not new. David practiced it:

Why are you downcast, O my soul?
  Why so disturbed within me?
Put your hope in God,
  for I will yet praise him,
  my Savior and my God.

[20]D. Martyn Lloyd-Jones, *Spiritual Depression: Its Causes and Cure*, (Grand Rapids, Mich.: Eerdmans, 1965), 116–117.

My soul is downcast within me;
   therefore I will remember you . . . (Ps. 42:5–6)
When my heart was grieved
   and my spirit embittered,
I was senseless and ignorant;
   I was a brute beast before you. . . .

My flesh and my heart may fail,
   but God is the strength of my heart
   and my portion forever. (Ps. 73:21–22, 26)

David reminded himself of the truth of God's presence and unchanging character, when his own feelings were at war with him and with God. This is especially vital when God has removed the awareness of his presence from our experience.

Likewise Asaph reminds himself and the Israelites that God is there even when he seems to be absent:

Your path led through the sea,
   your way through the mighty waters,
   though your footprints were not seen . . .

You led your people like a flock
   by the hand of Moses and Aaron. (Ps. 77:19–20, emphasis added)

In the midst of the terror of the Red Sea crossing, with the noise and tremor of two walls of water enveloping them, God was there, even though his "footprints were not seen."

Again, in the Lord's admonition through the prophet Isaiah:

Who among you fears the LORD
   and obeys the word of his servant?
Let him who walks in the dark,
   who has no light,
trust in the name of the LORD
   and rely upon his God. (Isa. 50:10, emphasis added)

In the words of one sage, "The child of the light is sometimes found walking in darkness but he goes on walking."[21] And during such dark times of the soul, we must talk to ourselves, reminding ourselves of the truth about us and the truth about God.

This need for the truth is especially relevant in an age such as ours which is so driven by passion. We want to *feel* God's presence; *feel* our commitment to him; *feel* good about our relationship with him. But God sometimes takes away what feelings we have and prevents others from sprouting. During these storms of the soul, he wants us to talk to ourselves about him. He desires that we "fear him" in the dark by recalling things he has told us in the light.

Job did all of these things, yet he still did not completely hold up. Why? I think it was because there are times when God deliberately pushes us *beyond* the strength we can muster by recalling his dealings with us in the past. I think God wanted more for Job, and through him, more for us today.

Refining Our Faith, Not Enlarging Our Faithfulness

The purpose of Job's suffering is nowhere recorded in the book. Yet it is possible to glean some likely intentions on the part of God by what is *not* stated. God never rebukes Job for a lack of faithfulness. Quite to the contrary, he twice calls him a "blameless and upright man, one who fears God and shuns evil." At the close of the book, he accuses Job's friends of misrepresenting God with the words (to Eliphaz), "I am angry with you and your two friends, because you have not spoken of me what is right, *as my servant Job has*" (Job 42:7, emphasis added). It is quite obvious from the way the book opens and closes, that what happened in between

---

[21]D. Martyn Lloyd-Jones attributes this statement to J. C. Philpot (*Spiritual Depression*, 17).

had nothing to do with a lack of faithfulness on the part of Job. God did not try Job in order to make him more faithful.

Rather, God wanted to purify Job's faith. Consider the words of the apostle Peter centuries later:

> In this you greatly rejoice, though now for a little while you may have had to suffer grief in all kinds of trials. These have come so that your faith—of greater worth than gold, which perishes even though refined by fire—may be proved genuine and may result in praise, glory and honor when Jesus Christ is revealed. (1 Peter 1:6–7)

There is a great deal of misunderstanding about the nature of faith, and this clouds our appreciation of the value of Job's suffering. We tend to assume that God simply wants to "enlarge" our faith, so that we become men and women of "great" faith. We believe that God wants to "toughen us up," so that we can endure even more difficult trials in the future, much like improving our time in the mile run. Nothing could be further from the truth.

God is committed to enlarging our understanding of him, of seeing more of *who he is*, not to enlarging our ability to believe he will behave in a certain way. Of course an enlarged sense of confidence in God is the fruit of an enlarged understanding of him, but we must not be deceived into thinking that God's goal is Christians who are more confident and assertive. In that case, a subtle shift occurs in which I actually have faith in my faith, rather than in God. This is the essence of "positive thinking" or "possibility thinking," and it has little or nothing to do with genuine biblical faith.

A description of genuine faith, the type that God longs for and labors to cultivate in each of us, is captured for us in the words of Job himself at the close of the book:

> Then Job replied to the LORD:
>
> "I know that you can do all things;
>   no plan of yours can be thwarted.

> You asked, 'Who is this that obscures my counsel
>   without knowledge?'
> Surely I spoke of things I did not understand,
> things too wonderful for me to know.
>
> "You said, 'Listen now, and I will speak;
>   I will question you, and you shall answer me.'
> *My ears had heard of you*
>   *but now my eyes have seen you.*
> Therefore I despise myself
>   and repent in dust and ashes." (Job 42:1–6, emphasis added)

In his affliction, Job wrestled with what he knew of God. It forced him to think through what was true about God. And in the process, Job had to seek God for understanding, because his own as well as that of his friends had failed him. Finally, Job realized that the proper question to be asked during suffering is not, Why? but, Who? Obtaining an answer to the why question places the burden on us—to live with whatever answer we are given. Seeking an answer to the *who* question drives us to God, and places the burden of sustenance and nurture where it belongs—on him.

The other option for Job would have been to turn his back on God, or in the words of his wife, to "curse God and die!" But Job didn't. He strove with all his heart to know and understand the Lord. And this is precisely what God wanted. It is a proven principle that comfort makes us slothful in our spiritual lives; prolonged ease tends to make us indifferent toward God and our need of him. God knows that suffering will either drive us to him or away from him. His desire, of course, is that we would strive to know him better:

> Whenever God slew them, they would seek him;
>   they eagerly turned to him again. (Ps. 78:34)
>
> It was good for me to be afflicted
>   so that I might learn your decrees. (Ps.119:71)

"You will seek me and find me when you seek me with all your heart." (Jer. 29:13)

One of the greatest ironies of the Christian faith is that some of the most precious times of fellowship with God are in the midst of intense pain and difficulty. This is because when our own resources finally fail us, God becomes to us what he should have been all along—our only sufficiency. Unfortunately, because of our abhorrence of pain and our misconceptions about faith, we often are quick to seek a cure rather than the Physician himself. In the words of G. Campbell Morgan (speaking of a statement made by Elihu):

> The reason why men do not find God is that the motive of their prayer is wrong. It is a cry for help rather than for God Himself.[22]

One of the primary purposes of God in the life of Job was that Job would grow in his understanding of the Lord. And Job's confession, "My ears had heard of you but now my eyes have seen you," is testimony that he had indeed learned what God wanted him to learn.

Facing the Unavoidable

A second valuable truth that emerges from the pain of Job's experience is that suffering is an inescapable part of the warp and woof of life. In 14:13–14, Job speaks of the unavoidable nature of suffering and pain; later, he states the focus of his hope for relief from life's pain:

---

[22]Morgan, *An Exposition of the Whole Bible,* 216.

> I know that my Redeemer lives,
>   and that in the end he will stand upon the earth.
> And after my skin has been destroyed,
>   yet in my flesh I will see God;
> I myself will see him with my own eyes—
>   I, and not another.
> How my heart yearns within me! (Job 19:25–27)

Job states clearly that he looks *forward* for his relief from suffering and pain, rather than looking for that relief within his present surroundings. Paul echoes this forward-looking attitude, while acknowledging that pain will be part and parcel of our lives until Christ returns:

> All this is evidence that God's judgment is right, and as a result you will be counted worthy of the kingdom of God, for which you are suffering. God is just: He will pay back trouble to those who trouble you and give relief to you who are troubled, and to us as well. This will happen when the Lord Jesus is revealed from heaven in blazing fire with his powerful angels. (2 Thess. 1:5–7)

The words of Job and of Paul stand in stark contrast to the spirit of a culture that runs from discomfort and demands to be massaged when pain is unavoidable. We should not, of course, be unhealthily infatuated with suffering. But we *should* be willing to acknowledge that suffering is normal in a fallen world. Our hope as believers is in the deliverance that will be ours when Jesus returns. Our responsibility in the meantime is to approach suffering in the present the same way Job did—with honesty, and with the determination to let it accomplish its cathartic work in our hearts.

Suffering for Others

Another purpose in the suffering of Job was beyond his comprehension, because it involved you and me and the countless others who have been enlightened, encouraged, and refreshed by his story. If Job had not endured suffering, and recorded his crushing experiences, *our* lives would be that much the poorer. Many Old Testament saints were told that their prophetic ministries were actually serving those yet unborn:

> It was revealed to them [the prophets] that they were not serving themselves but you, when they spoke of the things that have now been told you. (1 Peter 1:12)

Likewise, much of what God's people *suffer* is for the benefit of those whose lives they will intersect on life's highway:

> Praise be to the God and Father of our Lord Jesus Christ, the Father of compassion and the God of all comfort, who comforts us in all our troubles, so that we can comfort those in any trouble with the comfort we ourselves have received from God. (2 Cor. 1:3–4)

Edith Schaeffer sees this process clearly exemplified in Job's suffering:

> Job himself doesn't know what is going on in the battle, nor does he have any idea of the revolutionary understanding which his story will open up for future generations. *His* trials and tribulations, *his* agonies and struggles, *his* longing for death, and *his* trust in God will mean much to those who will follow.[23]

My own depression began to take on a meaningful shape as I studied the life of Job. I owe much of the understanding that came during that trial to the bewilderment Job experienced during his! We, not Job, are the real beneficiaries of Job's pain. And others, rather than ourselves, may very well be the beneficiaries of our pain. This is a difficult truth to ponder in an age characterized by self-absorption rather than self-sacrifice. But it is one of God's primary purposes in allowing us to suffer. Understanding this truth

---

[23]Edith Schaeffer, *Affliction* (Old Tappan, N.J.: Revell, 1978), 55–56.

can provide some sense of meaning when we are called by God to walk in darkness.

Learning From Job

A number of valuable lessons for dealing with pain, both ours and that of those we love, emerge from Job's experience. Probably the most obvious lessons can be distilled from the many dialogues between Job and his supposed friends.

The first is that we should seek to remain silent in the face of others' pain. We Christians seem to feel an intense pressure to say something profound to those who are hurting. And often we cause more pain than we relieve. Job's friends sat in silence for an entire week before they spoke, and the book is a record of their individual and corporate failure from that point on. We too need to remain still in the presence of those who are suffering. We must resist the temptation to provide an "answer," or an explanation for their suffering. The greatest support we can provide is often simply our presence; it communicates that we care deeply.

A second lesson from the failure of Job's friends is that speaking truthfully *about* God is not the same as speaking truthfully *on behalf of* God. A careful study of the multitude of exchanges between Job and his friends will reveal that much if not most of what they said about God was true. However, it was *not* true in *Job's* situation. God certainly punishes the wicked and rewards the righteous. But to conclude that all tragedy is a punishment for sin or that all blessing is a reward, is short-sighted at best. The only formula God is bound to follow is his own character. And within that circumference, he has great liberty. When we presume to speak on behalf of God, we sit in the seat of the prophet. And the most crucial criterion for a true prophet of God is accuracy. It is no small thing to presume to be a prophet. Shortly before he was martyred, the apostle Paul reminded Timothy of the importance of "correctly handling the word of truth" (2 Tim. 2:15). That charge is relevant to anyone who seeks to minister to the needs of others.

A third lesson from the failure of Job's friends is that, we should help those in pain to focus on what is true, but we should not negate the validity of their feelings. Job's friends never acknowledged Job's anger, depression, and despondency. Instead, they simply judged it as sin. Because Job was a "blameless and upright" man, one who "feared God and shunned evil," we can be assured that he, more than they, was aware of his sin. He did not need to be reminded of what he already knew. Rather, Job desperately needed someone to help him recall what he had *forgotten*—namely that he was the beloved child of a faithful God. We too need to acknowledge the feelings of those who are suffering, rather than accusing them.

What does Job teach about how to handle our *own* suffering? Probably the most important lesson is the necessity to continually remind ourselves of the truth when our hearts tells us otherwise. Paul's admonition in Philippians 4:8 is a sure antidote for the thoughts of fatalism and defeat that prey upon those in pain:

> Finally, brothers, whatever is true, whatever is noble, whatever is right, whatever is pure, whatever is lovely, whatever is admirable—if anything is excellent or praiseworthy—think about such things.

One of the most vital ways to survive the darkness of God's perceived absence, is to immerse ourselves in his Word, memorizing its promises and reminding ourselves of its truths. Our own thoughts will fight to free themselves from the circumference of God's revealed truth. We must do all that we can to guarantee that our conclusions are products of reflection on what God has said, not what we have felt.

Job's journey into darkness was the product of God's deliberate plan. It was not, however, the scheme of some demented deity who revels in seeing people squirm under pressure. It was the thought-ful plan of a loving God, intended to refine a man whom he dearly loved and to instruct a multitude of others yet unborn—including you and me.

ELEVEN

Jonah:
Pride and Anger

Sometimes, we can become depressed, defeated, or discouraged as a result of our own emotions, rather than because of circumstances or other people. Because our feelings are totally subjective, and become visible to ourselves and others only through our behavior, it is often difficult to isolate exactly which emotion is responsible for feelings of discouragement. Further complicating matters is the cause-and-effect relationship that often exists among our various emotions. For instance, what we perceive as anger may have had its origin in hurt feelings. Even depression itself can be a byproduct of a prolonged struggle with feelings of anger or hurt. And our anger can sometimes be traced to a perceived violation of our own pride. Such was the case with the Old Testament prophet Jonah.

Jonah is one of those rare biblical characters that everyone, even nonbelievers, has heard of. This is surely due to of the nearly incredible details that surround the story of his life—because there is really very little mention of him in the Bible. Other than the book that bears his name, there are only three references to him in Scripture. Nonetheless, "Jonah and the whale" go together much like Kermit and Miss Piggy in the minds of many children, so entrenched is this biblical character in the world of children's stories.

But Jonah is not merely a figment of someone's fertile imagination. He is a real historical character whose life is worth examining.

We first meet Jonah in 2 Kings 14:25. This verse is very helpful because it provides some vital information that is lacking from the book of Jonah itself—a reliable date for when he lived. In this verse, Jeroboam II, the son of Nebat, has just become king of the northern kingdom of Israel:

> He was the one who restored the boundaries of Israel from Lebo Hamath to the Sea of the Arabah, in accordance with the word of the LORD, the God of Israel, spoken through his servant Jonah son of Amittai, the prophet from Gath Hepher.

We can discern from the above passage that Jonah lived around 200 years after King David, in the ninth century B.C. We learn Jonah's father's name and his hometown.

We also read about Jonah in Matthew 12:39–40. In this passage, the Pharisees are demanding a "sign" from Jesus to validate his authority. Jesus' response is that he will give them no other sign except for the "sign of Jonah." He says, "For as Jonah was three days and three nights in the belly of a huge fish, so the Son of Man will be three days and three nights in the heart of the earth."

This passage is crucial because it establishes beyond a reasonable doubt that Jonah was a real person. There are those who say that Jonah is just a myth, the product of a vibrant Jewish imagination. Others say the story is merely an allegory, designed to teach that God loves the ungodly. Yet in this passage, Jesus is basing the factual reality of his impending resurrection on the existence of Jonah. You cannot build "proof" of something in the real world by linking it to a mythical person or event. Jesus clearly accepted Jonah as a historical figure. We can do no less.

Matthew 16:4 contains the final reference to Jonah. It is nearly identical to the statement Jesus made in Matthew 12:39. This is the extent of the biblical data we have on the prophet Jonah, yet most Christians are more familiar with him than they are with other biblical figures for whom we have reams of information. Why? I think it certainly is because of the supernatural nature of his mission, but more so, I believe it is because Jonah stands out in the pages of the Bible as a colossal failure. And we are less intimidated by fellow strugglers than we are by those who are great successes. Jonah is human, and we appreciate that.

Even though the biblical data on Jonah seems scanty, there is actually quite a bit that we can ferret out. First of all, Jonah was a "prophet." In 2 Kings, he is called, "the servant of God," and Jesus calls him a prophet. This is important because we need to realize from the outset that *Jonah was in the ministry.* He wasn't like the shepherd Amos, whom God called away from his work for one specific task. Jonah was accustomed to hearing God speak; he was familiar with doing the will of God. Jonah had a relationship with God; he *knew* Jehovah. From a superficial reading of the book of Jonah, we could get the impression that God appeared to this man and said, "Go here and do this," and Jonah disobeyed. But the truth is, Jonah and God had "worked together" enough before for him to earn the title, "servant of God." Others recognized that Jonah was God's man. He was no stranger to God or to the people of Israel, when it came to acting on behalf of Jehovah.

Actually, there *is* ample evidence in the book of Jonah itself that Jonah and God were far from strangers. In Jonah 4:1–2 we read, "But Jonah was greatly displeased and became angry. He prayed to the Lord, 'O Lord, is this not what I said when I was still at home? That is why I was so quick to flee to Tarshish. I knew that you are a gracious and compassionate God, slow to anger and abounding in love, a God who relents from sending calamity.'" The phrase Jonah used to describe God's character in this passage is almost a direct quote from Exodus 34:6, the classic Old Testament passage in which God responds to Moses' request to see the glory of God. The phrase, "a gracious and compassionate God, slow to anger and abounding in love" is God's own description of his character and nature. In fact, this is one of the very first appearances of such a lucid description of God as a God of love and compassion rather than merely a God of judgment. And this description comes from the mouth of the Lord himself.

What does Jonah's quoting this description tell us about *Jonah?* It tells us that Jonah was familiar with God's revelation of himself in the past, which means that he was familiar with the Scriptures. Jonah was familiar with the Word of God, but he was also apparently well acquainted with God himself, to be able to isolate those particular truths about God in the context of what God had asked him to do—preach judgment to a pagan nation.

This is all very important, because we need to have as accurate a picture of Jonah as possible before we can truly appreciate his life. Jonah was a man who knew God quite intimately; had served God faithfully; and, through his knowledge of the Scriptures, was familiar with God's dealings with mankind in the past. In short, he was qualified, trained, and experienced to do the very thing God was asking him to do. But instead of obeying God's call, this time the prophet runs.

Tracing Jonah's Disobedience

In chapter 1, God calls Jonah to go to Nineveh, and we read that, "Jonah ran away from the LORD and headed for Tarshish" (v. 3). Most scholars think that Tarshish was near Spain; Nineveh was on the Tigris River, north of present-day Baghdad. In other words, Tarshish was nearly at the opposite end of the known world from Nineveh! Jonah wasn't simply refusing to obey, he was actually trying to make his obedience impossible!

It was in the seaport city of Joppa, between Nineveh and Tarshish, that Jonah apparently made his choice to run away from the Lord and head for Tarshish. Joppa is the same place where the apostle Peter had his vision about going to preach to the Gentiles (Acts 10). It is a strange irony that eight centuries after Jonah's disobedience, another Jew would be facing the same challenge in the very same place. Perhaps Peter pondered Jonah's choice as he was making his own.

We can also see Jonah's resolute determination to disobey in his response to the sailors on the ship he boarded. God had already determined that Jonah *would* be going to Nineveh, so he caused a great storm to arise. The sailors were in a frenzy trying to discover who was to blame for the storm. When they cast lots and the lot fell to Jonah, they queried him about his part in their plight. Jonah instructed them to throw him overboard to still the storm. Do you think this was a heroic act of selflessness on Jonah's part? The runaway prophet fully expected to *die* in the ocean! That is how resolute he was about disobeying. If God was going to chase him, he would simply end the chase.

But God appointed a "great fish" to swallow Jonah. God is turning up the heat, to motivate Jonah to reconsider his decisions. The second chapter of Jonah contains his prayer of repentance, his deliverance from the great fish, and his subsequent decision to obey God's call. But I believe that Jonah did not pray this prayer until very near the end of his three-day stay-over in the fish. I believe Jonah hoped that he would simply die in the fish! Yet just as God had protected his wayward prophet in the storm, he protected him in the midst of what should have been another fatal environment.

Can you imagine what was going through this man's mind? First he thought he could run away from God, and he ended up running into him instead. Then he tried to allow himself to be killed, and that also failed. Now he's inside a giant fish, probably waiting to die there too. But nothing happens. Eventually, Jonah "cracks" and gives in to God.

Considering how hard Jonah tried to escape, it is very probable that even when he did go to Nineveh and preach, he did it without any sense of genuine passion and concern. I suspect that he put as little effort as possible into his call to repentance. From every observable shred of evidence, we have a man who obeyed as a last option, and performed without any sense of burden to do so. He was motivated by fear of punishment, not by love for the lost.

But why was Jonah so adamant about not going to Nineveh? What could possibly have driven a man to the place where he would rather die than obey?

Nineveh: Pagan Headquarters of the Known World

Nineveh, capital city of the nation of Assyria, was about 400 miles inland from the Mediterranean Sea. So when we read that the "great fish" spat Jonah up on shore, we must realize that he didn't just vomit him up on the outskirts of the city. It was probably at least a two-week journey, on foot, from the coast to Nineveh. The prophet had plenty of time to think, on his way to preach.

The Assyrians were a savage and heartless race of killers. They were the "professionals" when it came to world conquest. It was common for them to construct pyramids of human skulls outside the walls of cities they had conquered. They sometimes skinned people alive and hung the skins on the walls of Nineveh. Even the city was intimidating. Its walls were wide enough to drive three chariots around on top, side-by-side! We learn from Jonah himself that walking across the city was a three-day journey. It was an immense city populated by ruthless pagans—not your ideal place for friendship evangelism! So if *fear* was Jonah's reason for not wanting to go to Nineveh, it is fully understandable.

Fear, however, was not the reason. Jonah's reason for not wanting to go to Nineveh was pride. This becomes apparent in chapter 4.

Jonah has completed his assignment, and the whole city, from the king on down, has repented and turned to God. The Lord turns back from destroying an entire city of pagans because they have turned their hearts toward him. In what should have been exciting circumstances and cause for great rejoicing, "Jonah was greatly displeased and became angry. He prayed to the LORD, 'O LORD, is this not what I said when I was still at home? That is why I was so quick to flee to Tarshish. I knew that you are a gracious and compassionate God, slow to anger and abounding in love, a God who relents from sending calamity.'" (4:1–2)

Jonah is angry with God at a time when most evangelists would have been delirious with joy. Why? Why is he so upset in the face of an outpouring of God's grace? Simply because God had spared the city! Because of what he knew about the character of God, Jonah had been convinced that if he obeyed God, the Ninevites would be spared. So, rather than see a pagan nation turn to God, he had tried to run away.

Of course there were other dynamics at work here besides Jonah's parochialism. It is highly unlikely that Jonah would have returned home from Nineveh to a "ticker-tape parade"! Assyria was the rising power that would eventually crush the Jews, and surely the Jews already saw the handwriting on the wall. Jonah may even have been viewed as a traitor—as one who had betrayed the national interests of Israel. Surely that thought was circling in his heated mind. But the essential driving force behind his anger is pride. "I didn't want to go because I knew that if I did, you'd spare them. And I didn't want that. They're pagans! They're not your people!"

And in this final chapter, Jonah's anger follows the course that most anger follows—he becomes deeply depressed.

Tracing Jonah's Depression

As chapter 4 opens, we discover that Jonah is "displeased" with God's decision regarding Nineveh. And his displeasure degenerates into intense anger. Three times in the first nine verses, Jonah tells God that death would be preferable to life. God asks him twice if he feels he has a right to be angry. The first time, Jonah ignores him. But the second time he says, "You bet I do!" Angry people always feel that their anger is justified. To be unjustly angry would be an indication of immaturity, and no one wants to admit to that.

Jonah then goes outside the city, makes himself a little shelter and waits "to see what would happen to the city" (v. 5). Now, why would he do this? I believe Jonah really thought there was a possibility that God would change his mind *when he saw how distraught Jonah was!* The city has already repented, God has already relented, and yet Jonah sits, waiting to "see what would happen to the city." Depressed people often want the world to notice their discomfort . . . and adjust accordingly. Jonah seems to have thought there was at least a possibility that God would change his mind and destroy the city . . . just to ease *Jonah's* discomfort!

We can laugh at such a notion, yet how many times have *we* waited for others to notice our irritation, anger, or discouragement? How many times have we hoped that our friends would change their plans to adjust to our depression? How many times have we wished that the world would rearrange itself around our pain? Jonah's conduct, while extreme, is not unusual.

While Jonah is outside the city nursing his own wounded pride and anger, God "provided a vine and made it grow up over Jonah to give shade for his head to ease his discomfort, and Jonah was very happy about the vine" (v. 6). This is the only place in the entire book where Jonah is happy. And, not surprisingly, it's because his own discomfort has been alleviated. Even here, we see God attempting to minister to the brooding prophet so that he can teach him a larger lesson about his love and compassion. But while Jonah willingly accepts God's provision for *him*, he refuses to acknowledge the validity of that same grace and mercy for the Ninevites.

This "we-they" mentality is very common among angry people. When I constantly focus on my own "rights" and the violation of those rights, I quickly divide the whole world into two groups of people: those who honor my rights; and those who infringe upon them. There is very little middle ground. And in the case of Jonah, both God and the Ninevites were in the second group.

But how did Jonah migrate from displeasure as the chapter opens, to despair at its close? We can work our way backward, tracing Jonah's emotional steps to the actual cause of his depression. There are three visible emotional states, and one invisible attitude that provide us with clues.

Jonah's initial emotion, the one that launched him on the downward spiral, was resentment. Chapter 4 opens with the statement that, "Jonah was *greatly displeased* and became angry." Resentment is a predictable response when things don't go "our way." Jonah's whole life had taken a turn that he didn't like from the very beginning. He hadn't wanted to go to Nineveh in the first place; his attempt to run away had been thwarted; "Plan B," to die at sea, had fizzled; finally he had been coerced to preach a message he didn't like, to a nation he didn't love. Now, he was living with the fruit of his frustration: a repentant nation of pagans that he wished were dead. Jonah did not approve of the "script" God had written, and even less of the part he had been forced to play. He was "greatly displeased" with what God had planned for him and the Ninevites.

Jonah's resentment had taken root when God first told him to go preach to the Gentiles. He was the first Old Testament prophet to be given such an assignment. God asked him to do something he did not want to do. And eventually, Jonah had to come to terms with the reality that God *would* get him to do it, whether he liked it or not! Jonah felt "trapped" in the will of God. And it is very, very easy to become resentful when we feel trapped.

There have been a number of times when I have felt overwhelmed with the task of my own ministry, and have longed to be doing something else. Yet upon assessing my credentials, education, and experience, the "options" always seemed to evaporate. Slowly there grew the realization that unless something unexpectedly fell into my lap, I would have to stay put. Quite honestly, there have been times when I have continued in teaching simply because I had no options. Having lost sight of God's goodness, I wrestled repeatedly with resentment, which is always the result when we turn our gaze away from God's character. I, like Jonah, fought back anger against God for what he had asked me to do.

In Jonah's case, as is always true with unchecked resentment, the resentment turned to anger. Jonah had plenty of time to think about what had happened, what God had "done" to him—the inconvenience; the humiliation; the injustice. Jonah had been upset, but now he was mad!

At least Jonah was honest about his anger. He was angry with God, and told him so. Too often, we try to sidestep our anger with God by directing it toward some person—a spouse, an employer, a fellow motorist. Although it was unfounded, Jonah's anger was at least directed in the proper direction—toward God himself.

It is worth noting that Jonah's anger did not manifest itself in fits of rage or emotional outbursts. We sometimes fail to recognize our own anger or that of others because we are looking for tangible expressions, physical reactions, verbal explosions, or open hostility. Much anger is internalized, quiet and passive. Beneath a calm exterior may be a heart that is raging. But its rage, though masked, is evidenced by high blood pressure, arthritis, ulcers, or insomnia. Jonah was simply sitting on the hillside on the outskirts of town. He wasn't pacing the countryside, wringing his hands and shouting.

He wasn't throwing dust into the air or cursing the Ninevites. He was just sitting. Yet he *was* extremely angry.

Finally, Jonah's anger turned inward and became depression; he wanted to die. This degeneration of his outlook is understandable and normal, because extended anger takes a tremendous toll on us both physically and mentally. One of the unfortunate but inevitable physical consequences of anger is the constant presence of adrenaline in our bloodstream. Anger actually taxes our system, because the purpose of adrenaline is to elevate our body's ability to handle danger. It heightens our pulse and blood pressure, diverting blood flow to needed areas as well as initiating muscle tension. Consequently, there is a natural "let down" when the effect of the adrenaline passes. God designed this protective feature to occur at short intervals spaced relatively far apart. But in the case of *prolonged* anger, adrenaline is present on a nearly constant basis, depleting our body's strength and stamina over time. And as we saw with Elijah, physical fatigue is a natural precursor to emotional decline.

Anger eventually produces a sense of depression in those who nurse it. Jonah had most likely begun nursing his anger months before when God first told him to go to Nineveh! When his well-laid plans collapsed, it only added fuel to the fires of his fury. Jonah most likely *arrived* in Nineveh angry. It is probably inaccurate to think of him as suddenly "exploding" with anger on the outskirts of the city. Jonah's anger had been churning and smoldering for at least two weeks while he walked to his destination. It is unreasonable to think that he spent all that time preparing his message!

(Here's an encouraging aside: Jonah obeyed the *demands* of God while disregarding the *heart* of God. He preached out of fear for his own security, not concern for theirs. Yet God used Jonah, and can use us, in our disobedience. Even in our resentment, anger, and depression, God can use us to accomplish his will. While this truth must never become an incentive to disobey, it is nonetheless encouraging to those of us who feel like failures most of the time.)

The book of Jonah concludes with a masterful refutation by God of Jonah's reason for being angry. Jonah has reluctantly obeyed, and then retreated to the outskirts of the city, hoping against all odds that God would change his mind and destroy the Ninevites. While waiting, he constructs a makeshift shelter to provide a measure of relief from the blistering wind and sun. God, still attempting to elicit a repentant change in the prophet, provides a better shelter for the sulking saint in the form of a large plant.

However, in almost as little time as it takes to grow the vine, God destroys it. It is quite obvious that Jehovah is trying to remind Jonah that his own compassion knows no bounds and is not a reward for man's righteousness. Unfortunately, our depressed disciple doesn't get the point. In fact, he becomes even *more* angry at God—for destroying the plant!

Finally, God "crashes" Jonah's pity party with a few penetrating questions. First, God asks Jonah, "Do you have a right to be angry about the vine?" And Jonah retorts, "I do . . . I am angry enough to die." (4:9) Jonah believed his anger was justified. To respond otherwise would be to admit that it was sin. The book concludes with God's response to this statement.

God confronts Jonah with the truth of his self-centeredness. He says, "You have been concerned about this vine, though you did not tend it or make it grow." Jonah had done nothing to deserve God's provision of the vine, and he had done nothing to maintain its blessing. He merely enjoyed its shade. His only concern was what the plant did for him. In essence, God says, "Jonah, the only thing you care about is yourself! You don't care about the city, its inhabitants, its children, or even its cattle!" God rightfully confronts Jonah with the stark reality of his resentment. He had become so obsessed with his own rights that he was actually unable to feel any compassion or concern for a city of nearly a half million. However he *was* very concerned about the vine that had been eaten by worms during the night and could no longer provide him with shade! God makes it clear to Jonah that he has no right whatsoever to be angry.

God holds this truth before Jonah's face: His anger is the consequence of his obsession with himself, nothing more. It was the violation of his plans, his wishes, his feelings that brought on the resentment that turned to anger. Jonah wanted the world to revolve around himself.

Jonah had become especially upset when God asked him to do something distasteful and unpopular. How many times have we found ourselves mad at God for moving us to a new city, or putting us in a position we didn't want to be in? How often has our focus narrowed so as to accommodate only ourselves? Our resentment over the plan of God can blossom into anger and bear the fruit of depression just as surely and quickly as Jonah's did.

Twentieth-century Americans, perhaps more than any other people at any other time in history, are self-absorbed. We have magazines dedicated to "Self," seminars on improving our image of ourselves or others' images of us. Fitness crazes and diets abound. We are obsessed with improving, developing, asserting, babying, and massaging ourselves. Yet it also appears that, more than any other generation in history, we are unhappy and depressed! And this is as true for Christians as it is for those outside the faith.

I see this repeatedly in the lives of many of my students. Most come from comfortable, middle-class Christian homes. Their needs are met, and they daily enjoy sound and relevant Bible teaching at our school. Yet many of their lives seem empty. They have no sense of "mission" in life, focusing instead on the routine of daily existence. And as is always the case with God's people who have forgotten why we're here, their gaze has slowly shifted from others to self. Their *own* sense of comfort and happiness grows from a preoccupation to a vocation.

On the other hand, I have also seen high school students virtually come alive when they have tasted genuine participation in ministry, or have become involved in some way with the message of reconciliation.

Why? Why is it that, at a time in history when we have more information about God than at any other time, and more access to people who can help us in our discouragement, we are unhappiest? The number of Christians who are discouraged, defeated, or simply disinterested is staggering. The general mood of our culture right now is one of extreme anger. Why? Most likely for the same reason that Jonah was unhappy and depressed. He was self-absorbed. And we have seen clearly the end-product of that type of obsession. It is resentment, anger, and finally depression.

Jesus said in Luke 9:24, "For whoever wants to save his life will lose it, but whoever loses his life for me will save it." While Jesus is most likely referring primarily to our commitment to him, I think he is also stating an inviolable law of life: If I make self the focus of my passions, time, and energy, I will eventually end up with nothing. The life of Jonah testifies to the truth of this law. One of the reasons so many Christians are angry and depressed is because they have put their own "rights" ahead of others' needs. Jesus was a man for others, not a man for himself. When he speaks of us "losing" our life for him, he means living our lives in a way that is similar to his—for others.

When we choose to live for ourselves and our own "needs" and desires, it kills us spiritually and eventually even emotionally. When I choose to live for self, I will become resentful when my perceived needs go unmet; I will become angry toward those who failed to meet them; and eventually I will find little value in life itself. This was the path Jonah trod, and it will just as surely characterize our lives if we follow his example.

Near the close of the book of Isaiah, God provides a valuable counter-principle to this "law of death" so vividly seen in the life of Jonah. This is one of the Bible's clearest antidotes for the depression of self-absorption:

"If you do away with the yoke of oppression,
  with the pointing finger and malicious talk,
And if you spend yourselves in behalf of the hungry
  and satisfy the needs of the oppressed,
then your light will rise in the darkness,
  and your night [RSV, *gloom*] will become like the noonday.
The LORD will guide you always;
  he will satisfy your needs in a sun-scorched land
  and will strengthen your frame.
You will be like a well-watered garden,
  like a spring whose waters never fail." (58:9–11)

If we will pour ourselves out for the needs of *others*, God will minister life to us. We will discover that our own needs are met in the process of seeking to meet the needs of those around us.

Jesus said it even more simply: "It is more blessed to give than to receive" (Acts 20:35). The word "blessed" here has to do with personal happiness and fulfillment. To state it another way, "The way to self-fulfillment is self-sacrifice." Of course this is not to say that we should rush out and become as busy as possible. That would be a contradiction of everything we learned from the life of Elijah. But the tendency within the church today is to massage, nourish, and pamper the self, to the neglect of those around us. And such a view is not only contrary to the entire message of the gospel, it is also the surest way to personal unhappiness and depression.

Jonah's universe was centered in himself— *his* ideas, *his* felt needs, and *his* perspective on how things ought to be. When his life took a different turn, one he had not planned, he quickly grew resentful. His resentment turned to a consuming and costly anger, which eventually robbed him of the little joy of living that was left. When self becomes our focus, depression is inevitable. It is never a question of "if" we will become depressed, only *when*.

TWELVE

Jesus: Facing Rejection

Our egos are fragile and delicate warriors in an often hostile environment. Our ideas are challenged, our values questioned, and our faith assaulted. Each encounter introduces the very real threat of someone refusing to accept us for who we are. All of us face some type of rejection from time to time, but few of us will ever have to endure what the man in the following story experienced:

> He began his life with all the classic handicaps and disadvantages. His mother was a powerfully built, dominating woman who found it difficult to love anyone. She had been married three times, and her second husband divorced her because she beat him up regularly. The father of the child I'm describing was her third husband; he died of a heart attack a few months before the child's birth. As a consequence, the mother had to work long hours from his earliest childhood.
>
> She gave him no affection, no love, no discipline, and no training during those early years. She even forbade him to call her at work. Other children had little to do with him, so he was alone most of the time. He was absolutely rejected from his earliest childhood. He was ugly and poor and untrained and unlovable. When he was thirteen years old a school psychologist commented that he probably didn't even know the meaning of the word "love." During adolescence, the girls would have nothing to do with him and he fought with the boys.

Despite a high IQ, he failed academically, and finally dropped out during his third year of high school. He thought he might find a new acceptance in the Marine Corps; they reportedly built men, and he wanted to be one. But his problems went with him. The other marines laughed at him and ridiculed him. He fought back, resisted authority, and was court-martialed and thrown out of the marines with an undesirable discharge. So there he was—a young man in his early twenties—absolutely friendless and shipwrecked. He was small and scrawny in stature. He had an adolescent squeak in his voice. He was balding. He had no talent, no skill, no sense of worthiness. He didn't even have a driver's license.

Once again he thought he could run from his problems, so he went to live in a foreign country. But he was rejected there too. Nothing had changed. While there, he married a girl who herself had been an illegitimate child and brought her back to America with him. Soon, she began to develop the same contempt for him that everyone else displayed. She bore him two children, but he never enjoyed the status and respect that a father should have. His marriage continued to crumble. His wife demanded more and more things that he could not provide. Instead of being his ally against the bitter world, as he hoped, she became his most vicious opponent. She could outfight him, and she learned to bully him. On one occasion, she locked him in the bathroom as punishment. Finally, she forced him to leave.

He tried to make it on his own, but he was terribly lonely. After days of solitude, he went home and literally begged her to take him back. He surrendered all pride. He crawled. He accepted humiliation. He came on her terms. Despite his meager salary, he brought her seventy-eight dollars as a gift, asking her to take it and spend it any way she wished. But she laughed at him. She belittled his feeble attempts to supply the family's needs. She ridiculed his failure. She made fun of his sexual impotency in front of a friend who was there. At one point, he fell on his knees and wept bitterly, as the greater darkness of his private nightmare enveloped him.

Finally, in silence, he pleaded no more. No one wanted him. No one had ever wanted him. He was perhaps the most rejected man of our time. He ego lay shattered in a fragmented dust!

The next day, he was a strangely different man. He arose, went to the garage, and took down a rifle he had hidden there. He carried it with him to his newly acquired job at a book-storage building. And from a window on the sixth floor of that building, shortly after

noon, November 22, 1963, he sent two shells crashing through the
head of President John Fitzgerald Kennedy.

Lee Harvey Oswald, the rejected, unlovable failure, killed the
man who, more than any other man on earth, embodied all the success, beauty, wealth, and family affection which he lacked.[24]

Oswald's story is so tragic it borders on comedy—sort of like an
extended "Ziggy" cartoon strip. The rejection he endured was
extreme. Few if any of us will ever face such hostility from others.

But each of us will have to face some rejection, sometime. And
if we are not fully equipped to confront it, rejection can plunge us
into discouragement and depression.

Fortunately for us, God has faithfully provided extensive help
in the Bible regarding the difficult task of facing rejection. And it
can be found in a careful study of the One who "was despised and
rejected by men, a man of sorrows, and familiar with suffering."
(Isa. 53:3). Our Lord Jesus Christ faced and endured rejection of
the most extended and severe proportions. Yet his life is also virtually saturated with truth, insight, and healing balm for those of us
who have faced or will face rejection. Although Jesus endured rejection in all its fury and pain, he never surrendered to it.

Rejection and the Man of Sorrows

Our Lord's rejection actually began long before the Cross. Very
soon after the fall of man in Eden, God's redemptive plans were
set in motion to counteract mankind's basic hostility and antipathy
toward God. If it is true that man's heart is hostile to God, it is true
also that his hostility is manifest most clearly toward those who
represent God—especially toward Jesus Christ, God in the flesh.

---

[24]James Dobson, *Hide or Seek* (Old Tappan, N.J.: Revell, 1974–79), 17–18.

The first visible sign of Christ's rejection occurred with the announcement of his birth to King Herod by the Magi, and their subsequent decision to keep the Savior's birthplace a secret from Herod: "When Herod realized that he had been outwitted by the Magi, he was furious, and he gave orders to kill all the boys in Bethlehem and its vicinity who were two years old and under, in accordance with the time he had learned from the Magi" (Matt. 2:16). Before Jesus had reached his third birthday, he was already despised and hunted by the king of his own people! Jesus was perceived as a "threat" to Herod's power base. Insecure leadership is always threatened by competence, especially if it is accompanied by popularity. Sometimes, people will reject us if they perceive that we are a threat to their job security or their popularity.

This is as much the case in Christian organizations as it is in the business world. A charismatic and vibrant "newcomer" is often viewed with great suspicion and even criticism because he or she is a threat to the status quo. Herod was threatened by the thought that Jesus Christ could be a king.

It is interesting to note that it was Herod's hostility toward Jesus that drove Jesus and his family to Egypt and eventually to Nazareth, where Jesus spent his childhood and early adult years.

After growing up in relative obscurity in Nazareth, the day of Jesus' public ministry arrived. It was time to reveal to his people his true identity as the long-awaited Anointed One of God. After being asked to read Scripture in his hometown synagogue one Sabbath, Jesus announced to the congregation that he was the Messiah. He then went on to insinuate that their own spiritual condition was similar to the Jews of Elijah's day—stubborn and sinful! The residents of Nazareth were furious at such a claim. "They got up, drove him out of the town, and took him to the brow of the hill on which the town was built, in order to throw him down the cliff" (Luke 4:29). Not exactly what most young preachers long for as a response to their first sermon! Can you imagine how it would feel to be rejected by the people you had grown up with for thirty years; your neighbors, your peers, and your parents' friends? Jesus was rejected here because he told his own people the truth about themselves. For those who are comfortable in their spiritual lives, a confrontational message is never welcome, nor is the one who brings it.

His rejection at Nazareth forced Jesus to move on once again. It is interesting to see how he was being "extruded" into the very plan of God by means of the rejection of others. Sometimes, when God needs to move us on, he does so by making our present environment less than desirable.

The rejection Jesus experienced grew each year. On one occasion, Jesus' disciples ate some grain while walking through a field on the Sabbath. The religious leaders were offended by his obvious refusal to abide by their interpretation of the Sabbath laws. In a synagogue later that day, Jesus healed a crippled man's hand right before their eyes. Their response to this act of compassion is startling: "Then he said to the man, 'Stretch out your hand.' So he stretched it out and it was completely restored, just as sound as the other. But the Pharisees went out and plotted how they might kill Jesus." (Matt. 12:13–14)

Jesus' rejection by the religious leaders was due at least in part to the fact that he was unconventional; he didn't do things the way they did. For the Pharisees, tradition had achieved the status of Scripture itself. When Jesus challenged their self-righteous legalism, they promptly rejected him. Sometimes, challenging *why* people do a certain thing in a certain way is interpreted as a challenge to their authority in general. And to the Pharisees, who valued their religious system more than the truth, Jesus was a threat. They desired to subjugate people; he wished to set them free. They were driven by the letter of the Law; he sought to uphold the spirit of the Law. They believed in routine; Jesus was motivated by need. They were traditionalists; he was a non-conformist. Jesus didn't "fit," and therefore he was rejected.

After his rejection at Nazareth, Jesus established a new base of ministry operations in Capernaum, the hometown of Peter. Jesus preached what has been called the "Bread of Life" sermon at the synagogue in Capernaum. He called for a high level of commitment to him, using the imagery of "eating his flesh" and "drinking his blood." He spoke of himself as the "bread that came down from heaven," the bread that would enable people to live forever (John 6:57–58). After listening to this stirring sermon, we learn from John that, "From this time many of his disciples turned back and no longer followed him." (v. 66)

There is a rejection that can come when we ask others to commit themselves fully to Jesus Christ. Like those in Capernaum who enjoyed Jesus' wonderful teaching, the warm fellowship of friends, and the miraculous provision of food and health, there are many today whose only attachment to Christ is the weak link of enjoying the benefits of faith. When talk of serious discipleship occurs, they are suddenly disinterested, and those who preach such a message are unpopular and rejected.

My eldest son was at a sleep-over at a friend's house for his birthday. As the evening wore on, the boys decided to watch a rented video. About fifteen minutes into the movie, my son remarked, "Ya know, I'm not sure that the Lord would sit and watch this with us."

The mother was so moved by what Ben said that she turned off the movie. However, much to my son's dismay, that was the last overnight he was invited to. His honesty with his friends had a high price tag. And sadly, nearly three years later, he's still paying for it.

We can also be rejected by those outside the faith, when we seek to draw them into a relationship with Jesus Christ. We can be rejected by the very ones we are trying to win to Christ when we finally share the message of salvation with them.

One has to wonder what Jesus must have thought about his daily interactions with people. The Pharisees rejected Jesus because he was too "loose" in his interpretation of and obedience to the Law (Luke 6:1–11). The Jews in Capernaum rejected him because he was too strict and demanding in his requirements for his followers (John 6:25–66). In light of such reactions his words in Matthew 11 take on fresh meaning:

> "To what can I compare this generation? They are like children sitting in the marketplaces and calling out to others:
>
> > 'We played the flute for you, and you did not dance;
> > we sang a dirge, and you did not mourn.'
>
> "For John came neither eating nor drinking, and they say, 'He has a demon.' The Son of Man came eating and drinking, and they say, 'Here is a glutton and a drunkard, a friend of tax collectors and "sinners."' But wisdom is proved right by her actions." (vv. 16–19)

Being misunderstood, criticized, and rejected by people *over* us is painful and difficult to cope with. But it is made tolerable by the fact that we usually have a small band of faithful family members or friends who can provide some healing balm for our wounded hearts. Yet for our Lord, even these normal spheres of warmth had grown cold and hostile. Rejection is always painful, but there is an injury of deeper and more lasting proportions that results when even family members refuse to acknowledge our faith in God. Jesus' own half-brothers not only rejected his claims to be the Messiah, they actually taunted him about what they believed were his "delusions of grandeur," and encouraged him to act in a fashion they knew could cost him his life:

> After this, Jesus went around in Galilee, purposely staying away from Judea because the Jews there were waiting to take his life. But when the Jewish Feast of Tabernacles was near, Jesus' brothers said to him, "You ought to leave here and go to Judea, so that your disciples may see the miracles you do. No one who wants to become a

public figure acts in secret. Since you are doing these things, show
yourself to the world." For even his own brothers did not believe in
him. (John 7:1–5)

Jesus had said earlier in his ministry that his *true* brothers and
sisters were those who "hear God's word and put it into practice"
(Luke. 8:21). So, although the rejection by his biological siblings
stung deeply, Jesus could always rely upon those who had become
his closest friends during the three years of public ministry—his
twelve disciples.

Or could he? The biblical record paints a portrait of an increasingly complete rejection as the life of the God-man moves toward
its dramatic conclusion.

The most obvious and well-known rejection Jesus endured in
his last hours was from the hand of Judas Iscariot. For thirty pieces
of silver, he betrayed the Son of God into the hands of those who
had rejected him earlier—the religious leaders (Matt. 26:14–16).
Following the obvious rejection of Judas came three more significant denials that same evening. After filling their bellies in the
upper room, the remaining eleven disciples followed Jesus across
the Kidron Valley to the Mount of Olives, a familiar place of fellowship, worship, and rest. In the early morning hours of Good
Friday, Jesus told eight of his followers to stay and rest and then
asked the three who were his closest friends—Peter, James and
John[25]—to accompany him farther into the recesses of the lonely
garden, saying, "My soul is overwhelmed with sorrow to the point
of death. Stay here and keep watch with me" (Matt. 26:38). Jesus'
personal emotional pain at this point cannot be put into words.
His own description, "overwhelmed with sorrow to the point of
death" gives us a mere glimpse of what he must have been feeling

---

[25]These three men were with Jesus at the Transfiguration and a variety of other very
special occasions, giving the distinct impression that they had a special place in the
Savior's heart and plans.

and thinking. Luke the physician gives us the added insight that the capillaries in Jesus' face had apparently ruptured, mingling blood into his sweat glands, turning his very perspiration into a bloody testimony of a heart on the edge of bursting. (Luke 22:44)

Put yourself in Jesus' place. You are with your three closest friends in your darkest hour yet. And what is their response to your pain?

> Then he returned to his disciples and found them sleeping. "Could you men not keep watch with me for one hour?" he asked Peter. (Matt. 26:40)

I wonder if the psalmist's words nearly ten centuries earlier coursed through Jesus' mind at this moment: "Scorn has broken my heart and has left me helpless; I looked for sympathy, but there was none, for comforters, but I found none" (Ps. 69:20). Although this was not a deliberate attempt on the disciples' part to neglect the obvious needs of their friend (they were tired and had full bellies), nonetheless, it was rejection.

Not all rejection we face is hostile, deliberate, and malicious. There is also a rejection of neglect. You have probably endured it yourself, and most likely caused it as well. There are times when we are at a loss for words, so we say nothing. We are at a loss for what to do, so we don't act at all. And there are times when we are so preoccupied with our own pain that we do not see and hear the overt or subtle cries for help from those we love. Whatever the cause, it is perceived as rejection by those in need. In this case, Jesus felt deserted by those he was counting on at a moment in his life when he needed them very much.

Our Lord's experience of rejection now began to spread like a drop of ink in a glass of water. Following this encounter with the three sleeping friends, Jesus faced alone the hostility of the temple guard . . . as all eleven of his fearful disciples scattered into the garden shadows (Matt. 26:56). The neglect of three accelerated to abandonment by all. Jesus was alone with his enemies. I believe that his sense of abandonment and rejection by men was near its apex at this moment.

Yet it was not over. One final human rejection from those he loved lay ahead for Jesus—a clear and personal rejection from the one who had confessed earlier, "Even if I have to die with you, I will never disown you" (Mark 14:31):

> Now Peter was sitting out in the courtyard, and a servant girl came to him. "You also were with Jesus of Galilee," she said.
>
> But he denied it before them all. "I don't know what you're talking about," he said.
>
> Then he went out to the gateway, where another girl saw him and said to the people there, "This fellow was with Jesus of Nazareth."
>
> He denied it again, with an oath: "I don't know the man!"
>
> After a little while, those standing there went up to Peter and said, "Surely you are one of them, for your accent gives you away."
>
> Then he began to call down curses on himself and he swore to them, "I don't know the man!"
>
> Immediately a rooster crowed. Then Peter remembered the word Jesus had spoken: "Before the rooster crows, you will disown me three times." And he went outside and wept bitterly. (Matt. 26:69–75)

Jesus' world of support was gone. He had been rejected—by neglect, abandonment, and denial—from every quarter where he had once known respect, love, and support. He was alone in a sea of humanity that hated him. The rejection of man continued throughout the night and into the next day. He was mocked by passing crowds of Jews, his brethren by race (27:22–25). The Roman soldiers beat him, offered blasphemous worship, and spat on him (vv. 27–31). Finally, the very religious leaders who had demanded his blood jeered him in his agony on the Cross, accusing him of fraud and failure (vv. 41–43). His rejection from man was complete. For the moment, it appeared that there was no remaining corner of the universe from which hostility, hatred, or indifference could emerge. Yet, as he neared the end of his earthly mission, the harshest rejection of all was still awaiting our Lord.

Cloaked in mystery and truth that defies explanation, is the unavoidable fact that Jesus Christ experienced some form of genuine rejection from his own heavenly Father. In the incarnation God had become man, and on the Cross, this incarnate Son of God took upon himself the sins of the humanity he had adopted. In the words of Paul, "God made him who had no sin to be sin for us, so that in him we might become the righteousness of God" (2 Cor. 5:21). And one of the inevitable consequences of this eternal redemptive transaction was that God forsook his only Son:

> From the sixth hour until the ninth hour darkness came over all the land. About the ninth hour Jesus cried out in a loud voice, *"Eloi, Eloi, lama sabachthani?"*—which means, "My God, my God, why have you forsaken me?" (Matt. 27:45–46)

In his darkest hour, alone among men, Jesus Christ suddenly found himself looking at the Father's back instead of into his face.

Jesus experienced rejection for what he *did*, for who he *was,* and for who he *was not.* He endured abandonment and ridicule by his family. Neglect and denial from his closest friends and "business associates." He was mocked by his neighbors and perfect strangers. He was spurned by the rich and poor alike. He even experienced a genuine rejection by his own Father—God himself.

Lessons From the Man of Sorrows

On the night of his arrest, Jesus told his disciples that they should not expect to be treated any better than he had been treated while on earth (John 15:20–25). That means, quite simply, that the rejection Jesus experienced is illustrative of what we can expect.

A number of very obvious truths about rejection emerge from the life of Jesus.

The rejection Jesus knew was in part a consequence of being misunderstood. His own family and even the disciples failed to comprehend the true nature of his identity and mission. All of us have faced this type of rejection. It is frustrating. It is obviously the product of *others'* misconceptions rather than of *our* misbehavior. Somewhere deep in our heart is the gnawing thought that we could straighten this out if only we had the opportunity or time. Jesus' family and followers simply were not seeing the bigger picture of who he was and why he was here. Probably all of us have at times been misjudged and rejected by Christians who either misunderstood something we said, or believed, without question, comments made by others about us.

Another factor contributing to our Lord's rejection, especially from the "religious establishment," was that he was very unconventional. The Pharisees had created a world of predictable order and protocol. Their traditions had slowly achieved the status of truth. Their methods were not merely adequate, they were the "right" way to do things. Jesus drew their criticism because he not only challenged their rules, but questioned their motives—something no one had dared to do for decades. People are suspicious of novelty, particularly if it makes them question or evaluate themselves. Unconventional people make us nervous because they make us think about who we are, what we do and, more importantly, why we do it. You and I can expect to be rejected if we dare to follow Christ wholeheartedly . . . because the way of the Cross is so counter to the way of the world.

Although being unconventional and misunderstood can kindle rejection from others, there is a more basic reason why Jesus faced such continual and intense rejection. It was because he was a righteous man. He exhibited the character of God in every area of his life—the very thing you and I are supposed to do (1 Peter 1:16).

Jesus made the connection between personal holiness and rejection clear early in his ministry when he said, "Blessed are those who are persecuted because of righteousness, for theirs is the kingdom of heaven" (Matt. 5: 10). The relationship between rejection and righteousness is a bright thread running throughout the tapestry of God's Word. Jesus summarizes the battle between the righteous and the unrighteous throughout the entire Old Testament in his scathing attack on the self-righteous Pharisees:

> And so upon you will come all the righteous blood that has been shed on earth, from the blood of righteous Abel to the blood of Zechariah son of Berekiah, whom you murdered between the temple and the altar. (Matt. 23:35)

Paul told Timothy bluntly that, "Everyone who wants to live a godly life in Christ Jesus will be persecuted" (2 Tim. 3:12). It was Jesus' honesty about the Pharisees' hypocrisy that prompted them to reject him. It was his righteous demands for Lordship that incited the Jews in Capernaum to quit following him. It was the possibility of personal harm that was responsible for his disciples deserting, even denying him when he needed them most. It was his unwillingness to condemn sin in others that drew hatred from those who felt righteous in themselves.

Righteousness is the character of God. It is as unconventional as God himself. It demands a higher standard from those who feel self-confident. It exercises mercy upon those who are overwhelmed with guilt. It judges all men equally. Jesus was God in a body, and those who stood before him had to either admit that, or seek to ignore their own sense of shame. Many chose the latter, and rejected the Righteous One to preserve their own unrighteousness.

Make no mistake, Jesus lived with rejection partly because he refused to barter his integrity in the marketplace of popularity. And as uncomfortable as it is to admit it, rejection is inevitable for any who care to take the call of Christ seriously.

As you seek to manifest the character of God, you may even find rejection in the place you least expect it—from other Christians. As the world tightens its grip on the hearts and minds of God's people, those who seek to reflect the heart of God and espouse the values, lifestyle, and outlook of his kingdom may find themselves the target of criticism from other believers who want to maintain an attachment to the world and its goods. A life of righteous commitment is an unspoken indictment on a casual spirituality, and will undoubtedly attract criticism and produce rejection.

There is also ample evidence in Scripture that God, in his unsearchable wisdom and sovereignty, actually *wills* rejection for some of his children. The story of Joseph in Genesis 37–50 virtually pulsates with examples of rejection. His brothers, his employer, and his cell-mates in prison all rejected him. Yet as painful and unfair as Joseph's life appears to us, he captures the bigger picture when he says, "You intended to harm me, but God intended it for good to accomplish what is now being done, the saving of many lives" (Gen. 50:20). It is obvious, as Joseph's life concludes, that the rejection God allowed in his life was for his own good, and for the good of Israel and of all mankind. We, like Joseph, may experience rejection that is divinely orchestrated by the One who loves us—as part of his gracious plan to make us like him. Whether it is the rejection of a boss we simply cannot get to like us, or of another Christian who refuses to believe our account of a conflict, God has a plan that transcends our immediate pain.

The life of Jesus teaches us that rejection from others is an inevitable legacy of life in a fallen world. Being misunderstood, judged, and disliked is normal in a sinful society. A life of righteousness will be rejected by a world of compromise. Jesus faced it, endured it, and so must we.

But there's an additional phenomenon common to our experiences with rejection that Jesus *did not* exhibit. Jesus never became depressed because of the rejection of others. Even his statement in the Garden of Gethsemane, "My soul is overwhelmed with sorrow to the point of death" (Matt. 26:38), related to the task that lay ahead of him, not the rejection that surrounded him. Why does rejection often produce such intense discouragement and depression in us? What was there in the life of Jesus Christ that prevented him from deep discouragement about the rejection he faced? And what can we glean from God's Word to help us overcome this kind of depression?

Depression and Rejection

First we must grapple with the question, Why does rejection often cause us to become discouraged, defeated, or depressed? To answer that question, we go to the apostle Paul. Paul, like Jesus, had some firsthand experience with rejection. In fact, much of Paul's life was spent trying to *undo* the rejection he faced from within the church. Many early Christians refused to acknowledge that Paul was a bona fide apostle. His second letter to the Corinthians consists almost entirely of a defense of his apostleship.

One comment in this letter sheds valuable light on why we are so negatively affected by rejection. In attempting to convince the Corinthians that he is at least as competent as some of the men who were seeking to malign his reputation in Corinth, Paul says, "We do not dare to classify or compare ourselves with some who commend themselves. When they measure themselves by themselves and compare themselves with themselves, they are not wise" (2 Cor. 10:12). This last phrase, "they are not wise," literally means "to lose the ability to think clearly." In other words, Paul is saying that when people measure themselves by their peers (or by their peers' opinions of them), they lose the ability to think clearly.

Too often we believe that the approval of "significant others" is essential for our sense of worth and security. If those "significant others" do not provide us with their approval, or if they exhibit outright disapproval, we find ourselves feeling dejected and insecure.

This is why we are able to endure, perhaps even thrive, under the rejection of some people: *They* are not part of the group of "significant others" whose approval means so much to us. We are relatively unaffected, perhaps even delighted that *they* do not approve of us. The disapproval of such individuals can even provide a sense of worth, if we love the things they hate. This reverse perspective is at the root of much teen rebellion, when the teens welcome their parents' anger.

There seems to be an unwritten law on our hearts that the more significant the source of approval, the more significant we feel. Likewise, the more significant the source, the more significant the rejection. Oddly, it is usually we ourselves who determine who is "significant" and who isn't. So, under closer examination, *we are the ones ascribing worth to those whom we will allow to determine our own value!* As weak as this reasoning is, it holds powerful sway in most of our lives.

Rather than seek to refute this principle of approval by significant others, I would like to take it a step further. If it is true that the more significant the source, the more significant the approval, let's examine what the Scripture has to say regarding *God's* opinion of us:

> How great is the love the Father has lavished on us, that we should be called children of God! And that is what we are! The reason the world does not know us is that it did not know him. (1 John 3:1)

> For I am convinced that neither death nor life, neither angels nor demons, neither the present nor the future, nor any powers, neither height nor depth, nor anything else in all creation, will be able to separate us from the love of God that is in Christ Jesus our Lord. (Rom. 8:38–39)

The truth is, God himself loves us and "approves" of us in Christ! In the words of the apostle Paul, "But now he has reconciled you by Christ's physical body through death to present you holy in his sight, without blemish and free from accusation" (Col. 1:22). Approval from people means nothing. What counts is whether or not we have the *Lord's* approval: "For it is not the one who commends himself who is approved, but the one whom the Lord commends" (2 Cor. 10:18). If it is indeed true that the more significant the source, the more significant the approval, then we as Christians have the highest possible approval!

This is also why our Lord did not wilt under the continual rejection of people. He knew that he had his Father's approval—and that approval eclipsed all others. From the very beginning of his public ministry, Jesus had his Father's approval: "And a voice came from heaven: 'You are my Son, whom I love; with you I am well pleased'" (Mark 1:11). Jesus affirms this commendation from the Father when he says that, "On him [on Jesus himself] God the Father has placed his seal of approval." (John 6:27)

Jesus could endure the rejection of others, even the rejection of his close friends, because ultimately he knew that God the Father approved of him. You and I stand in the righteousness of Jesus. We share that same approval. The disapproval of others may anger us and perhaps even wound us, but we must remind ourselves, as our Lord did, that we are accepted by God. This seems simplistic, I know, but the truth is, when we base our sense of worth on the approval of others, we have "lost the ability to think clearly." The surest way back to clear thinking is to remind ourselves of the truth: God himself approves of us in Christ.

There's one more, very significant reason that we should not let rejection lead us into depression: The rejection Jesus Christ faced and endured was "substitutionary": It was for you and me! Isaiah's prophetic statement that, "He was pierced for our transgressions, he was crushed for our iniquities . . ." (53:5) has in view not just Christ's death, but also the fact that he was "despised and rejected by men" (v. 3). Jesus was rejected by men, so that *we* could be approved by God! Whenever you and I place our personal security and sense of worth in the bankrupt vault of human approval, we are minimizing—maybe even negating—a significant portion of Christ's sufferings on our behalf.

Rejection from others is unavoidable. It is real and painful, but it need not be the cause of serious discouragement. Jesus Christ not only bore a rejection he did not earn, he did it so that you and I could be approved by God.

There will be no escape from the rejection of people; but there will also never be a time when I am rejected by God.

THIRTEEN

Barnabas: Encouragement— The Alternative to Self-Preoccupation

We have examined several biblical characters who were discouraged and depressed due to circumstances, people, and attitudes that we discovered are the normal fare of life on a fallen planet. We have gleaned reasons for hope, strategies for growth, and insights for change from their failures, successes, and responses to God. In this final chapter, I want to put the spotlight on one last biblical figure; but I want to do so with a different agenda. As we come to the conclusion of *Wounded Saints*, I want you to digest the truth in this chapter not to help yourself, but to help others.

In this chapter we will study the life of a rather obscure New Testament figure who provides a role model for ministering to others in need. He is Joseph from Cyprus . . . but he is more popularly known as Barnabas.

Spotlight on Barnabas

Barnabas is another one of those biblical characters who just suddenly appears in the sacred record. He makes his rather abrupt debut in Acts 4:

> All the believers were one in heart and mind. No one claimed that any of his possessions was his own, but they shared everything they had. With great power the apostles continued to testify to the resurrection of the Lord Jesus, and much grace was upon them all. There were no needy persons among them. For from time to time those who owned lands or houses sold them, brought the money from the sales and put it at the apostles' feet, and it was distributed to anyone as he had need.
>
> Joseph, a Levite from Cyprus, whom the apostles called Barnabas (which means Son of Encouragement), sold a field he owned and brought the money and put it at the apostles' feet. (vv. 32–37)

From the very outset, Barnabas is presented as a deeply sensitive and compassionate man. The phrase, "whom the apostles called . . ." literally means that they changed his name from Joseph to Barnabas,[26] or Son of Encouragement. Surnaming, in Scripture, was normally done to highlight a particular quality or characteristic in one's life (for instance, Jesus changed Simon's name to Peter, which means "rock.") The implication is that the leaders in the Jerusalem church recognized that Joseph was an encourager of the saints.

That Barnabas was indeed an encourager is evident in this our first account of his interaction with others: He sold some of his personal property with the specific goal of meeting needs in the fellowship. It has been said that sympathy feels other people's pain, but compassion recognizes what will happen if a need is not met,

---

[26]The Greek word for *called* means "to surname," and the verb tense of the participle here indicates that this renaming had occurred at a specific time in the past.

and goes on to meet that need. Barnabas not only saw what was needed in the fellowship, he acted to meet the need. He was an enabler. This trait will reappear time and again as we study his life. In fact, as we learned in the Preface, the Greek word family from which the English word *encouragement* comes literally means to enable people to stand on their feet when, if left to themselves, they would surely collapse. Such was the earmark of the life and ministry of Barnabas.

Barnabas reappears five chapters later in the context of the conversion of Saul of Tarsus, the enemy of the church. And once again we see Barnabas' desire to reach out to others—in this case, Saul. But we also learn that the Son of Encouragement must have been highly respected and a man of credibility:

> When he [Saul] came to Jerusalem, he tried to join the disciples, but they were all afraid of him, not believing that he really was a disciple. But Barnabas took him and brought him to the apostles. He told them how Saul on his journey had seen the Lord and that the Lord had spoken to him, and how in Damascus he had preached fearlessly in the name of Jesus. (Acts 9:26–27)

Upon this man's word, the apostles accepted the validity of Saul's conversion, even though they were riddled with fear and suspicion. We must also assume that it was Barnabas who sought Saul out, listened to his story, and concluded that it was genuine; for in this passage it is *Barnabas,* not Saul, who is providing the account of the conversion! Barnabas was willing to take risks with people. He had all the same information as the rest of the church leaders, yet he deliberately chose to draw alongside Saul and do all that he could to help him deal with this very real difficulty in his life. As a result of Barnabas' ministry to Saul, the new convert secured a position of respect and love in the leadership of the early church. (See Acts 9:25, 30.)

We should also note, however, that Barnabas was not naive in his compassion. As we have seen, he must surely have spent time alone with Saul before taking the risk of bringing him into the fellowship. He most likely listened to Saul, asked questions of him, and made absolutely sure that this man was honest and sincere. He didn't merely jump thoughtlessly into a ministry situation, believing that because he was a Christian, it was his "duty." In our own attempts to help others we need to, in the words of Jesus himself, be "wise as serpents and innocent as doves" (Matt. 10:16). Many well-meaning Christians have found themselves taken advantage of or even abused because they were naive in their ministry to others. Barnabas was careful before he was fully caring. We would do well to follow his example.

Barnabas next appears in Acts 11, when the Jerusalem church sends him north to Antioch to investigate reports of Gentile conversions—something yet unheard of by the predominantly Jewish church. They were apparently convinced of Barnabas' ability to "see into the true nature of things," as had been so clearly evidenced in his recent dealing with Saul. This passage provides us with further insight about the ministry of Barnabas:

> When he arrived and saw the evidence of the grace of God, he was glad and encouraged them all to remain true to the Lord with all their hearts. He was a good man, full of the Holy Spirit and faith, and a great number of people were brought to the Lord.
> Then Barnabas went to Tarsus to look for Saul, and when he found him, he brought him to Antioch. So for a whole year Barnabas and Saul met with the church and taught great numbers of people. (Acts 11:23–26)

The Greek words for *encouraged them* indicate that Barnabas did this continually while he was in Antioch, not merely when he first arrived. It was an ongoing focus of his ministry. We also learn that there was real substance to his encouragement—Barnabas and Saul "taught great numbers" while in Antioch. Encouragement is more than a warm feeling. It has significance and purpose.

It is also worth noting that, in meeting the needs around him, Barnabas was not intimidated by the ministry gifts of other people. He traveled to Tarsus to recruit Saul to come help him minister. How often are we, by contrast, either envious of or threatened by other gifted Christians who stumble into the circle of "our" ministry! Barnabas knew no such fear. He was so focused on the needs of others that the vehicles of ministry did not matter.

One has to wonder if perhaps Barnabas' example of focusing on the end purpose of ministry, rather than on the means, influenced the young convert Saul to pen these words years later as the apostle Paul:

> It is true that some preach Christ out of envy and rivalry, but others out of goodwill. The latter do so in love, knowing that I am put here for the defense of the gospel. The former preach Christ out of selfish ambition, not sincerely, supposing that they can stir up trouble for me while I am in chains. But what does it matter? The important thing is that in every way, whether from false motives or true, Christ is preached. And because of this I rejoice. (Phil. 1:15–18)

Next in Barnabas' life is a brief trip to Jerusalem to deliver financial gifts, following which he brings his cousin, John Mark, back to Antioch.[27] It is at this juncture that God begins to set into motion the forces that will eventually launch Saul on the course of apostleship and notoriety.

The Temporary Nature of Helping Relationships

The Holy Spirit tells the church at Antioch to, "Set apart for me Barnabas and Saul for the work to which I have called them" (Acts 13:2). This is the commencement of a life of missions for both of these men, but it will also prove to be one of the last chap-

---

[27]Acts 11:30, 12:25, Col. 4:10.

ters of their missions partnership. They leave on what is now known as the "First Missionary Journey of Paul," going through Cyprus and parts of Asia. John Mark accompanies them on this first journey, but leaves midway through the trip to return home (v. 13). This first journey reveals a number of key insights regarding the ministry of encouragement.

God had used Barnabas to train Saul. It is obvious from the word order that Barnabas was the designated and recognized leader of this dynamic duo. In the book of Acts, from chapters 11–13, there are seven instances where Barnabas and Saul are mentioned together, and in every case, Barnabas' name is mentioned first. In fact in Acts 13:1, where the prophets and teachers of the Antioch church are listed, Saul's name appears *last* in a list of five, with Barnabas' name at the head. Up to this point, Barnabas is the mentor, Saul the student.

However, on the island of Cyprus, Barnabas' "hometown," something very significant occurs. From Acts 13:42 on, the majority of the occurrences of their names has the order reversed; Saul (known from here on as Paul) appears first, followed by Barnabas. I believe that sometime on this first journey, Barnabas slowly—perhaps even imperceptibly—slid out of the "spotlight" and allowed Paul to become the leader. This is very significant for our study.

We must realize that it was a *need* in Paul's life that brought the two men together in the first place. In fact, it was Paul's needs that provided the basis for the relationship. When those needs were met, however, the reason for the relationship was no longer there. Barnabas knew this, I believe, and he allowed the partnership to begin dissolving. I picture Barnabas more and more "behind the scenes," following-up Paul's ministry, rather than out in front setting the pace.

This is a crucial principle for those whose spiritual gifts or ministry are built around encouragement. It is absolutely essential that people with these gifts do not limit their friendships to the people they are helping. People like Barnabas will find themselves facing hurt and bitterness if they do not realize this basic principle of encouragement: When the need is met in the "helpee's" life, the basis for the helping relationship is gone. That is not to say that two people in such a relationship cannot or should not become and remain friends. But in many cases, when the helpee ceases to be dependent, he or she tends to "pull away" from the helper. If the helper does not realize the temporary nature of helping relationships, they may sustain unwarranted and unnecessary hurt when the relationship dissolves.

Issues or People?

The next major appearance of Barnabas is in Acts 15. Paul and Barnabas have been sent to the Jerusalem church to secure an answer concerning which Jewish laws, if any, Gentile converts should be expected to obey. Knowing what we do about Paul's uncompromising zeal for orthodoxy, it is very likely that *his* interests at this meeting were mainly in the arena of the issue itself— sorting out false doctrine from the truth. Barnabas, however, whom we already know was a "people person," probably saw the problem as a hindrance to the growth of these new Gentile converts. His motivation for seeking answers was totally different from Paul's. One wanted to resolve an issue, the other wanted to help people. Of course the passion for doctrinal purity that characterized Paul's life and ministry was necessary, but I believe that when it comes to the ministry of encouraging others, we need especially to follow Barnabas' example. Indeed the damaging effects of being totally "issues centered" are preserved for all time in this same chapter.

Near the end of Acts 15, Paul announces that he wants to return to the cities he and Barnabas had evangelized and visit the churches they had planted. Barnabas agrees to the idea and informs

Paul that he plans to bring his cousin, John Mark. Paul has other thoughts about John Mark:

> Barnabas wanted to take John, also called Mark, with them, but Paul did not think it wise to take him, because he had deserted them in Pamphylia and had not continued with them in the work. They had such a sharp disagreement that they parted company. Barnabas took Mark and sailed for Cyprus, but Paul chose Silas and left, commended by the brothers to the grace of the Lord. He went through Syria and Cilicia, strengthening the churches. (vv. 37–41)

Paul's choice of words for Mark's "desertion" is very strong, implying mild treason.[28] Paul simply had no time for anyone who had failed as miserably as John Mark had on their previous trip. To Paul the "issue" was as clear as crystal: Mark was not qualified to accompany them. Barnabas should be able to see the logic of Paul's choice. And, if he didn't see the logic, then they could no longer minister together.

Paul's unwillingness to give Mark a second chance surely confirms Paul's later description of himself as the "worst of sinners" (1 Tim. 1:15). Of all people, Paul should have been the first to see potential in someone whom others despised and mistrusted. Of all people, Paul should have been willing to give someone a second chance. For Paul himself had been the recipient of such Christian kindness years earlier, at the hands of none other than Barnabas, the man he now found himself in "sharp disagreement" with! Barnabas had believed in Paul when no one else did. Barnabas had been willing to give Paul another chance, to provide him with the opportunity to prove himself. Barnabas saw potential in a man everyone else hated. And Barnabas had been willing to risk his own reputation to rebuild Paul's. Now, when Paul has a chance to do the same—to be a "people person" rather than an "issues person"—he refuses.

---

[28]He uses the Greek word apostanta, from which we get our English word apostate.

But Barnabas, true to character as the "Son of Encouragement," simply ends his ministry of encouragement with Paul and begins it anew with John Mark. At this point Barnabas essentially fades from the pages of Scripture. Subsequent references to Mark, however, show that Barnabas was as committed and successful with his second disciple as he had been with his first. We note, for one thing, that this young man whom Paul judged to be an apostate went on to author the Gospel which bears his name. Secondly, we learn in 1 Peter 5:13 that Mark was a trusted companion of the apostle Peter.

Finally we find Paul himself, in prison awaiting execution, realizing deep in his soul that his rash criticism of John Mark had been unwarranted and wrong:

> Do your best to come to me quickly, for Demas, because he loved this world, has deserted me and has gone to Thessalonica. Crescens has gone to Galatia, and Titus to Dalmatia. Only Luke is with me. Get Mark and bring him with you, because he is helpful to me in my ministry. (2 Tim. 4:9–11)

Barnabas was a "people person" rather than an "issues person." I believe that if he had had to choose between what seemed "just" and what seemed "best," he would always have allowed his decisions to be tempered by how they would affect people. Paul, on the other hand, had to learn what Barnabas already knew. And in the gracious plan and timing of God, he did.

Barnabas, however, did not simply "ride off into the sunset" as a hero, in his decision to stick with John Mark. We would like to think that when we stand up for those whom others discard, God will openly reward us. Unfortunately, the work of encouragement, of "keeping people on their feet," may cost us the criticism of others. In Acts 15:40 we read, "But Paul chose Silas and left, commended by the brothers to the grace of the Lord." Paul, not Barnabas, received the commendation of the church at Antioch! This was the same church for which Barnabas had done so much in its early life (Acts 11:19–24). Indeed it was Barnabas who had first brought Paul to Antioch, where they had ministered side-by-side. Now, it seems, Barnabas is misunderstood, his judgment questioned, and his convictions rejected by the very people he had nurtured so faithfully. In choosing Mark, Barnabas lost the rest. Sometimes the ministry of encouragement to others can produce discouragement in us. But the cost is worth it, for John Mark, as we have noted, became the author of the Gospel of Mark.

One final aspect of being a "people person," illustrated for us in the life of Barnabas, needs to be highlighted. Unfortunately, it is a mistake we should learn from, not a strength we should emulate.

Some of what I am about to say is conjecture, based on inferences from various portions of the New Testament, but I believe quite strongly that it is true and significant. We know from our study so far that Barnabas was more concerned about people than about issues. And for the most part, that is a strength. However, there is an instance in Scripture in which Barnabas' attachment to people got him into trouble. Some background may be helpful.

In Acts 15, when Barnabas and Paul went to Jerusalem to determine how Gentile Christians should regard Jewish Law, it is interesting to note that Peter stood up and defended the Gentiles, using an argument that I could easily hear coming from the lips of Barnabas as well:

> After much discussion, Peter got up and addressed them: "Brothers, you know that some time ago God made a choice among you that the Gentiles might hear from my lips the message of the gospel and believe. God, who knows the heart, showed that he accepted them by giving the Holy Spirit to them, just as he did to us. He made no distinction between us and them, for he purified their hearts by faith. Now then, why do you try to test God *by putting on the necks of the disciples a yoke that neither we nor our fathers have been able to bear*? (vv. 7–10, emphasis added)

Peter doesn't argue primarily on the basis of theology. He builds his case on his experience with these people and the detrimental effect on them of maintaining a legalistic view of true spirituality. I would guess that Barnabas would have shouted "Amen!" to Peter's sermon that day. It is possible that he sensed a sort of camaraderie with Peter. If so, that would help explain Paul's later account of a serious error of judgment on the part of both Peter and Barnabas. The incident reveals a common weakness of people persons:

> When Peter came to Antioch, I opposed him to his face, because he was clearly in the wrong. Before certain men came from James, he used to eat with the Gentiles. But when they arrived, he began to draw back and separate himself from the Gentiles because he was afraid of those who belonged to the circumcision group. The other Jews joined him in his hypocrisy, so that by their hypocrisy even Barnabas was led astray. (Gal. 2:11–13)

Peter, because of his attachment to people, lost sight of the "issue" at a very crucial time. He acted in hypocrisy out of fear of rejection from those he respected. And, I suspect, Barnabas followed suit because of his association with Peter. In this incident, we see a very real danger for those gifted in encouragement—namely, the temptation to sacrifice their convictions about what is right and true for the sake of a relationship. This is just as real a danger as Paul's tendency to neglect the person in favor of the principle. True encouragers need to ask God to give them the wisdom and courage to avoid either extreme.

The Pattern of the Encourager

Reviewing the life of Barnabas, we can see a pattern to his ministry which can be of great value to us as we reach out to others:

1. The encourager spots someone with a genuine need and has a sense of how to meet it.

2. The encourager draws alongside this person with the goal of helping him grow.

3. The encourager gives sustained, faithful help.

4. The need is met.

5. The relationship either dissolves or changes into a genuine friendship, because the basis of the original relationship (the need) no longer is present.

6. The encourager spots another person in need, and the cycle begins all over again.

Simply knowing that this is a normal, predictable cycle in a helping relationship is absolutely vital. It will prevent the one giving the help from growing bitter or feeling used when (and if) the one helped slowly slips away. But more importantly, it will help keep our focus where it belongs in this type of relationship—on the other person and their needs, rather than on ourselves.

As I observed in the Introduction, it has been said that the smallest package in the world is someone wrapped up in himself. Much of the discouragement and depression that has such a strangle hold on the American church is due to the fact that we are spending more and more time trying to "fix" ourselves, and less and less time ministering to others. Isaiah's inspired comment nearly twenty-five centuries ago, to which we have been drawn twice already, provides a fitting close to this chapter, and indeed to all we have learned from the lives and teachings of these *Wounded Saints:*

"And if you spend yourselves in behalf of the hungry
    and satisfy the needs of the oppressed,
then your light will rise in the darkness,
    and your night will become like the noonday.

The LORD will guide you always;
   he will satisfy your needs in a sun-scorched land
   and will strengthen your frame.
You will be like a well-watered garden,
   like a spring whose waters never fail." (Isa. 58:10–11)